NIGERIA OJUKWU AZIKIWE BIAFRA BEYOND THE RISING SUN
BY
DR. S. OKECHUKWU MEZU

NIGERIA OJUKWU AZIKIWE BIAFRA
BEYOND THE RISING SUN
BY
DR. S. OKECHUKWU MEZU

ACKNOWLEDGMENTS

With full gratitude to all those who fought and died for the defense of freedom, justice and equity.

The following journals and books in which some of these articles or interviews were first published are gratefully acknowledged: www.blackacademypress.com; cpcimostate.org., igboville.com; Black Academy Review, nigerianworld.com.

Dedicated
To
All the Innocent Victims of the Biafra War
and to
ROSE URE MEZU, MY WIFE,
whom I left in Abidjan on her 21st birthday
ten weeks after our wedding
to return to war-torn Biafra on Ojukwu's invitation And
to Marcus Garvey who gave inspiration to the Biafra Flag Land
of the Rising Sun

NIGERIA OJUKWU AZIKIWE BIAFRA
BEYOND THE RISING SUN
BY
DR. S. OKECHUKWU MEZU

OJUKWU, BIAFRA, RISING SUN, NIGERIAN CIVIL WAR POGROM, POLITICS, IGBOS, CONFEDERATION, FEDERALISM AFRICAN POLITICS History Africa General History / Africa / General Nigeria Nigeria History Civil War, 1967-1970 Foreign public opinion Participation, Foreign Atrocities-History, Military history, Nigerian Civil War, 1967-1970

All Rights Reserved Including the
right of reproduction in whole or in
part in any form

Copyright   2012 by Black Academy Press, Inc.

Published by

BLACK ACADEMY PRESS, INC.
4015 OLD COURT ROAD
PIKESVILLE, MARYLAND 21208 USA

CONTENTS

1. Foreword: Weep Not for me but for Nigeria and our children. 9
2. Chief Samuel Onunaka Mbakwe And Dr. Michael Okpara in Nigerian Politics.............. 19
3. Dr. Nnamdi Azikiwe in Nigerian Politics 26
4. Chukwuemeka Odumegwu Ojukwu in Nigerian Politics...36
5. Inherent Desire to Thwart the Peoples Mandate in Nigeria's Political History 71
6. Nigeria's Se-Lection in 2007: Chronicle of Shame and Deceit. 85
7. Vice President Jonathan of Nigeria and National Assembly Resolution and the Transfer of Power.......... 91
8. Dr. S. Okechukwu Mezu Message to Nigerians In the Diaspora: Our Contract with Imo State 104
9. INEC and Supplementary Elections in Nigeria: The Case of Imo State 114
10. The Loud Drums of Civil War are Sounding in Nigeria: No Six Year Term for President and Governors 129
11. A Befitting Monument for Chukwuemeka Odumegwu Ojukwu...................... 133
12. Bibliography 147
13. About the Author 157

CHAPTER ONE
FOREWORD:
WEEP NOT FOR ME BUT FOR NIGERIANS AND OUR CHILDREN

It was never my intention to write a book on Chukwuemeka Odumegwu Ojukwu just as it was never the intention of Odumegwu Ojukwu to secede from Nigeria and declare the independent State of Biafra. But in life, convergence of circumstances create situations which shape the actions and reactions of human beings and in the process, a course of action is undertaken and history is created and when later this history is written, read and studied, it is often interpreted or misinterpreted as if it were an inevitable pre-determined and meditated course of action. This is not always the case.

This work had its genesis from an email from John Okiyi, a member of Igboville through one of my daughters, Dr. Nina Mezu-Nwaba to me: "*Good day Sir, Kindly pardon us for bothering you so soon. But this is surely an issue your insight is urgently needed. The attached is a discussion thread that is ongoing at Igboville. It seeks to compare Zik and Ojukwu as Igbo leaders. Along the line, it was suggested that Zik sabotaged us during the war and did nothing to actualize Biafra, or help prevent the massacre of our people in Northern Nigeria. The key will be to help educate us on what exactly Zik did for Ndigbo before, during and after the civil war. A similar perspective on Ojukwu will surely help us. Sir, kindly review the attached conversation and weigh in with a view that we can publish. It will really help to guide our members, especially the young ones. Thank you and God Bless You.*" John Okiyi Kalu. Igboville is a network of Igbo professionals in Nigeria and the Diaspora dedicated to creating a new and strong Igbo, based on mutual trust, dignity and unparalleled unity. This request was coming shortly after the group had asked me to weigh in on their discussions as to who was a better Igbo leader, Dr. Michael Okpara or Chief Samuel Onunaka Mbakwe, the first article in this compilation. I complied under pressure from my children. I suddenly also realized that the first of our eleven children was born in 1969 and knew little or nothing about the Biafra-Nigerian Civil War. They wanted to learn and needed to learn. John Okiyi wrote back on November 20, 2011 following the essay on Dr. Nnamdi Azikiwe: "*Thank you so much sir. We are eternally grateful to you. God bless you sir.*"

Well, thank you too and I am eternally grateful to all of you, the young and not so young - John Okiyi Kalu, John Obasi, Chukwuemekam Eric Chukwuemekam, Maxwell Ohtugo, Afikpo Chic, Paul Kalu, Chin Akano, Ndubuisi Ojimadu, Uchenna Ezima, Emeka Maduewesi and other members of Igboville group and to Kelechi Eme who first introduced me to the Igbo online community most especially to my daughter Dr. Nina Mezu-Nwaba who insisted and put pressure on me to respond to the yearning of the young for information. What I had suspected for long became more evident and apparent when I realized that the majority of Governors, National and State Assembly men and women were not born or were toddlers at the Independence of Nigeria in 1960. Some are filled with misconceptions not out of mischief but due to the dearth of firsthand accounts of our history and the absence of a reading culture in the country where books are extravagantly launched but never read. The young, ignorant of history, march headlong and obstinately into the bottomless quagmire of the Nigerian politics of the Sixties. If corruption then was basic and elementary, today, it is quadratic and exponential for those elected or selected to govern tend to see the State as their personal property. There is a definite difference between the State and the Government of a State. A state government that ruthlessly suppresses citizens' peaceful protest in support of freedom, justice and equity may unwittingly push its citizens over and into a Rubicon of blood and in the process vicariously become equally guilty of treason and felony against the State."

WEEP NOT FOR ME
BUT FOR NIGERIANS AND OUR CHILDREN

(Being partly the text of a New Year's message on January 1, 2012, to CPC colleagues, in Nigeria and the diaspora.)

Nigerians are generally aware of all the efforts made by the Peoples Democratic Party (PDP) Government of Nigeria to promote Justice Salami out of office as Head of the Court of Appeals before the Federal Elections of 2011. When eventually he was forcibly and illegally forced out during the pendency of the Presidential Election Tribunal under his headship, the result of the Presidential Election Petition was a foregone conclusion. The rest is an aberration of historic and judicial proportions.

General Buhari, you should remain undaunted and resolute as some of us are for the sake of Nigerians, our children, black Africa and the black world. Victory has never been handed on a platter of gold, not in sports and never in politics and people, fortunately, can never be fooled all the time or forever. You must not give up. We must, as like minds, continue to work together irrespective of religion and ethnicity. If Nigerian fails, then black Africa fails. We must not fail. We will not fail. We must not give up. We must continue to try. If we with all the intelligence, resources, exposure and experience at our disposal fail, then the millions of educated and non-educated unemployed Nigerian youth of today will be condemned to another fifty years of political servitude, judicial lawlessness and parliamentary brigandry.

The achievements - scientific, economic and infrastructural - of other countries, with less than ten percent of the population, human and material resources of Nigeria cry to the high heavens for justice, equity and good governance in Nigeria. The good Lord has given Nigeria so much in natural and human resources, yet there are no good roads, no water to drink, little or no electricity, a dying educational system, dilapidating infra-structure in all spheres of endeavor and activity whether by air, land and sea, or in the postal, health, commercial and industrial arena. We must strive for progressive change. The nation is dying and the present rudderless government is comatose. This has become very apparent to everyone, Nigerians and foreigners alike. This is not the time to retreat but the time to actively organize for change - change in the psychology of Nigerians, change in the attitude to governance, change in the administration of justice, change in the legislation and execution of laws.

You can always count on me and there are many others who feel the same way. We are in it together, and success is not a distant dream but a reality within reach. "

- *Dr. S. Okechukwu Mezu" - January 1, 2012*

SPONSORS OF INSECURITY IN NIGERIA

Who are the real sponsors of insecurity in Nigeria. Who are those actively creating the scenario for another civil war? We all are, by our actions and inactions, complicity and silence beginning with the government, encouraged by members of the Senate and the House of Representatives, and propagated by hordes of political and economic sycophants and parasites found in all strata of society - including Judges from the Supreme Court to the local customary and sharia court, Professors from the Universities to the local elementary school, business men from the public limited companies (PLC)s to the village outfits like Okonkwo Adeniran & Mohammed, Sons and Daughters Trading and Contracting Company. The Labor Union

Leaders are the worst offenders. They "break and quench" (like the myriads of old Tokunbo cars condemned in Europe that are imported to litter and adorn the decrepit roads in Nigerian towns and villages), forever riding on the support of the masses and abandoning them in the middle of the sea for their own selfish and personal aggrandizement.

No individual is wiser than the entire nation or even an entire village. The only way to avoid another Civil War in Nigeria is to call a National Conference of the component parts of the Nigerian Federation. There is a lot of sense in Warren Buffet's recent proposal (2012) for the United States of America. Some of us have for long advocated similar solutions for the problems of Nigeria as evidenced in some of these articles in this work.

1. Members of the National and State Assemblies should collect salaries while in office and should receive no pay when out of office. They should like other Nigerians participate in any existing contributory Retirement program available to the common people.

2. The notion that a Governor deserves a sinful N300,000,000.00 ($2 million US dollars) retirement home at the expense of the people (where the worker's monthly minimum wage was less than N10,000.00 cries to the high heavens for justice and equity).

3. Members of the National and State Assemblies and Governors and other public office holders should not be allowed to vote for themselves a pay raise and their pay should rise in tandem with any cost of living adjustment available to the ordinary Nigerian.

4. They should participate in the same healthcare system which should give them the added incentive to ensure that the healthcare system is adequate for their needs and that of the nation.

5. Representation in the National and State Assemblies should not be a career and should be limited like the terms of office of the President and the Governors to only two consecutive terms.

6. Serving Legislators should not be allowed to execute contracts in the guise of Constituency projects and should not be allowed to benefit directly as contractors for projects they themselves approved in the appropriation.

7. Better still, Legislative work should be a part time engagement attracting sitting allowances that do not collectively add up to more than the full time salary of the topmost civil servant, and if above, should not exceed it by more than fifty percent.

8. With these minor adjustments, politics will cease to be a "do or die" business that pays the Legislator several millions of Naira a month.

Recently there was a nationwide protest over the removal of fuel subsidy which is possibly the only decision made by President Goodluck Jonathan that I support but the timing was off and there should have been elaborate and visible preparation to get all the refineries working, roads improved, corruption in the oil sector controlled. But I fully supported equally the massive strike undertaken by Nigerian workers to protest against a government that does not have their interest at heart. As my wife, Dr. Rose Ure Mezu, wrote at the beginning of the fuel subsidy strike: *"So, now what can be done except what Nigerians are doing through street protests and boycotts. Except also that people are protesting the wrong cause -* ***fuel subsidy*** *rather than* ***loss of lives*** *- what does that say about our priorities? That we Nigerians as a people value material comforts more than human lives. To compound the confusion, it is an Igbo Finance Minister who is spearheading the Fuel subsidy removal which the Igboville recent write-up considers a distraction from the ongoing pogrom against the Igbos. The*

Igboville group accused the government: "Nigerian government is seemingly complicit with this terror group because they have not shown the will to combat and destroy it. Rather they have made deals with the terror groups in the past and actually offered amnesty to this terrorist organization," and this in the face of the fact that the Igbo states and Governors more than any other Group brought Jonathan to power in 2011. So, why does the President and his advisers not address the situation more effectively and decisively? And what does that say about the Igbos' ability to make good choices. Nigeria is a multi-ethnic polity and we can not live in isolation. It is about time to start making clear-eyed, politically realistic choices and not emotional and sentimental ones. It is time to strive to form more sensible, pragmatic collaborative political associations since every other group seems to fear Igbos equally."

It seems ironical that the Igbos will again be complaining to the world about another pogrom. Why complain to the world when Igbos know at the same time that a Christian Southerner was elected Head of the Nigerian Government through the bloated votes supplied by Igbo State Governors, and Igbos know further that an Igbo man is head of the Nigerian Army, an Igbo man Secretary to the Federal Government, an Igbo man the Deputy President of the Senate, an Igbo man the Deputy Speaker of the House of Representatives; an Igbo woman is Minister of Finance and another Minister of Petroleum Resources. There is no need to call upon the Israelis for help. The Israelis will not die for the Igbos just as no Igbo man has volunteered to defend the Israelis. The Igbos have all the help they will ever need. The Igbos alone can and will defend themselves. They will never be exterminated. Some of us insistently warned the Igbos during the last election in April, 2011 about the inevitable consequences of voting for Goodluck Jonathan, the protegee of Obasanjo who, unfortunately, still believes the Biafran War is not over and the Igbos still need to be subdued and enslaved . We can never abandon our people. But no one can lead a people who refuse to follow or to listen.

Other Nigerians like Chief Tony Momoh see the problems of Nigeria as a matter of structure: *"Then the other one is structure. We must restructure Nigeria because Nigeria cannot work as it is. The earlier we come to that, the better. So, when you say you want to change the Constitution, you are wasting your time because you are looking at the people who are changing the Constitution and who are not willing and can never agree to undermine themselves by robbing themselves of what they are enjoying. So, if you really talk of restructure, though we are talking of such fundamental restructuring that would make us look at what it is that we have today; 36 states of the federation, all of them are enjoying the same structural adjustment as the three regions were doing in 1960. So, we have a governor, a House of Assembly and then you have the civil service structure. It was three at independence, four in 1963 when the Mid-West was created; 12, then 19, 21, 30 and now 36. And it is the same structure. The abuse of that structure was reflected when the old Bendel State was split into two - Edo and Delta. They had 18 permanent secretaries when it was Bendel and when they split it into two, obviously, it ought to be nine permanent secretaries but Edo alone had 32 permanent secretaries. And each permanent secretary in Nigeria earns the same as his colleague anywhere in the country when we do not have a unitary civil service structure. We need change. But what I say now is that Muhammadu Buhari cried and a lot of people started saying he was shedding crocodile tears. But Buhari knew the corruption in this system. He knew the fraud and indiscipline in this system and he cried. That is manifesting now with what we have after removing oil subsidy"* [Tony Momoh , Sunday, January 15, 2012]

Finally, Nigeria is made up of various ethnic nationalities. None of the various nationalities should dissolve into the other or lose its specificity, whether cultural or religious, for the sake of a Nigerian nation. In the words of Chukwuemeka Odumegwu Ojukwu: "*I am a Nigerian. But I am also an Igbo. It is my being Igbo that guarantees my Nigerianness as long as I live. Consequently, my Nigerianness shall not be at the expense of my Igboness. The Nigerian nation must therefore work for all ethnic nationalities in Nigeria.*" This is not far removed from the words of Pierre Teilhard de Chardin, [L'Energie Humaine (1962)] who wrote in his book *Human Energy* "*Why do we hesitate to open our hearts wide to the call of the world within us, to the sense of the earth?...Men suffer and vegetate in their isolation; they need the intervention of a higher impulse, to force them beyond the dead point at which they are halted and propel them into the region of their deep affinity. The sense of the earth is the irresistible pressure which comes at a given moment to unite them in a common enthusiasm...The age of nations has passed. Now unless we wish to perish we must shake off our old prejudices and build the earth.*" To those who would like to see this as racism or tribalism, Leopold Sedar Senghor, apostle of Negritude would counter: "*Négritude... is neither racialism nor self-negation. Yet it is not just affirmation; it is rooting oneself in oneself, and self-confirmation: confirmation of one's being. It is nothing more or less than what some English-speaking Africans have called the African personality.*" For Senghor Négritude must take its place in contemporary humanism in order to enable black Africa to make its contribution to the "Civilization of the Universal," which is so necessary in our divided but interdependent world. This is true equally of the Nigerian nation. Igboness is neither racist nor tribalistic. It is neither racialism nor self-negation. It is an affirmation of a being, confirmation of oneself as a being. Igbo personality must take its place in contemporary humanism and Nigerian nationhood just like the individual personalitites of other nation groups in Nigeria. The Igbo person must bring its quiddity, to the collective called Nigeria. The Igbo person, like any other ethnic person, is neither a beast nor an angel. In the words of Blaise Pacal and Nicholas Machiavelli, "*Man is neither angel nor beast and the misfortune is that he who would act the angel acts the beast.*" Nigerian national politics should be the art of the survival of a people or a group of nations and not a revolutionary or dictatorial march into collective suicide.

CHAPTER 2

Samuel Onunaka Mbakwe and Michael I Okpara in Nigerian Politics

To: My dear daughter, Dr. Nina Mezu Nwaba:
This is a brief attempt to answer the question from Igboville which you sent to me: *"Please help me out here. A young friend of mine asked me who is the greatest governor of Igbo origin. Am torn between Chief Samuel Onunaka Mbakwe and Sir Michael Okpara. What do you think? Please give reasons for your position."* [John Okiyi, igbo.ville@yahoo.com].

They lived in different times and clime. Dr. Michael Okpara was the Premier of Eastern Nigeria (Today's South-Eastern states (Imo, Anambra, Abia, Enugu, Ebonyi) and parts of South-South states (Rivers, Akwa Ibom and Cross River). He was not elected but chosen over Barrister R. Amanze Njoku and Prof. Eyo Ita and leader of NCNC in the Eastern House of Assembly by Dr. Nnamdi Azikiwe who was heading back to the national scene Lagos preparatory to the Independence of Nigeria. The headquarters of Eastern Nigeria was at Enugu. There were initially three regions - Eastern Nigeria, Western Nigeria and Northern Nigeria. A fourth Region was added later, Mid-Western Nigeria, comprising present Delta, Edo and Bayelsa states more or less. Nigeria during Dr. Michael Okpara's time was a Federation and the Regions could exercise almost the full powers of a nation with the exclusion of non-concurrent powers like Defense & Police Affairs, External Affairs, etc.) Each Region depended mostly on internally generated revenue - East Nigeria on Palm Oil, Western Nigeria on Cocoa, Northern Nigeria on Groundnuts and their pyramids.

Dr. Michael Okpara was a strong, able, astute leader and more confrontational than Dr. Nnamdi Azikiwe, the former

Premier. Dr. Azikiwe handed over to Dr. Okpara and became Governor General, later ceremonial President, of Nigeria following Independence on October 1, 1960. Dr. Michael Okpara set up Adapalm which helped fund the establishment of the University of Nigeria at Nsukka, a Land grant institution modelled on the US Michigan State University system. It successfully challenged the University of Ibadan (formerly University College of Ibadan (UCI) then with Prof. Kenneth Dike as the Principal/President and Dr.E.C. Edoziem and the Dean of the College of Medicine. Michael Okpara's government set up among other industries Golden Guinea Breweries in Umuahia (Independence Brewery) one of the first in the country, Ceramics Industry, Umuahia. He and his colleagues Dr. Akanu Ibiam - Governor of Eastern Nigeria - (Afikpo), Prof. Eyo Ita (Calabar) Barrister R. Amanze Njoku (Emekuku), Dr. Jaja Nwachukwu (Ngwa), Justice C. J. Mbanefo (Onitsha) to mention a few ran a government of skilled intellectuals and professionals unlike today where touts and rabble-rousers dominate. They set up Government Colleges in Enugu, Owerri, Afikpo and Umuahia with the highest of standards and competition. Life was simple, food was abundant and cheap and farming was the main employer and the population was mostly rural. Under this regime, people were healthier and better than they are today. In the urban areas. where there was light, Electricity Corporation of Nigeria (ECN), it was steady, regular and reliable. The Post Office was efficient and mail from Nigeria to the United States was delivered reliably in one week to ten days. Scholarships to colleges and the Universities were provided to the few students then accommodated on the basis of excellence and need both on the Divisional, Provincial and Regional level. Dr. Michael Okpara supported General Ojukwu during the Biafra War, though during the end he genuinely disagreed (not openly) with the drafting of young, unprepared and poorly equipped Biafrans to the war front where some were mowed down by the better equipped Nigerian troops oiled and well-supplied by Britain and the Soviet Union. But unlike Dr. Nnamdi Azikiwe who defected to Nigeria, Dr. Okpara stayed with Biafra till the end and went on Diplomat missions for Biafra to France, Ivory Coast, Tanzania and Zambia whose governments Dr. Okpara heavily supported and funded during their struggle for independence. Dr. Okpara went into exile after the war and returned to Imo state before the 1979 elections. The roads in Eastern Nigeria were narrow, reasonably good then but lined on both sides by Oil Bean (Ugba) trees. Most were not macadamized but borrow pit earthwork maintained by a hard-working and dedicated crew of men each locally employed and assigned basically to each one mile of dirt road to fill pot holes and cut gutters to facilitate drainage and the run-off of water.

The regime of Dr. Michael Okpara was cut short by the *coup d-etat* of January 15, 1966 master-minded by Major Chukwuma Kaduna Nzeogwu, a brave, nationalistic and uncompromisingly ascetic first class soldier in thought, word and deed. During this coup the Premier of Northern Nigeria (Sir Ahmadu Bello), Prime Minister of Nigeria (Tafawa Balewa), Minister of Finance (Festus Okotie Eboh), Premier of Western Nigeria (S. L. Akintola) were killed amongst others. Dr. Michael Okpara was spared to the consternation of the rest of the country. General T. Aguiyi Ummunnakwe Ironsi, the most Senior Army Officer, and Igbo man, became President of Nigeria until the counter-coup that brought Colonel Gowon to power on July 29, 1966 and led to the killing of high ranking Igbo officers and Aguiyi Ironsi and his brave host Colonel Fajuyi as well as the pogrom and massacre of thousands of Igbo men, women and children in Northern Nigeria. The Civil War brought a concentration of power in the hands of central government of the "Federation" of Nigeria especially with the creation initially of twelve (12) states out of the existing four regions and more so with the establishment of the present thirty-six (36) states in the country.

Whereas Premier Michael Okpara ruled a larger group Eastern Nigeria at a time of peace and relative non-oil prosperity with some agitation then for the creation of Calabar-Ogoja-Rivers (COR) State, Samuel Onunaka Mbakwe was elected Governor of the Greater Imo State carved out of the then East Central State and comprising of today's Imo State, Abia State and parts of Ebonyi state (Afikpo and Ohaozara). Mbakwe took office after the marvelous rehabilitation of several schools by the East Central State Government of Colonel Ochefu, the creation of a wonderful master-plan for the Owerri Metropolis by the young and dynamic first Military Governor of Imo State (1976) Commander Ndubuisi Kanu who pioneered Divisional hospitals in every division. Ndubuisi Kanu was followed by the lazy, tribalistic, insensitive and unproductive government of Colonel Adekunle Lawal who virtually liquidated Imo State government treasury and assets. He was succeeded by the short-lived but purposeful and professional regime Colonel Adenihu who handed over to Governor Mbakwe on October 1, 1979. Colonel Adenihu was instrumental in the building of the Commissioners' Quarters (New Owerri) which he desperately tried to complete before handing over, the Construction of the State House of Assembly, the construction of the still uncompleted unit condos meant for Members of the State House of Assembly in New Owerri. In fact, Colonel Adenihu brought the Commissioners' Quarters to ninety percent completion by October 1979 but Mbakwe waited till the very end of his first term in 1983 before completing the remaining 10% at more than the cost of the original building because of inflation.

On assumption of office the Government of Mbakwe received like other states an unexpected Federal Allocation of N79 million Naira (then a windfall) which he immediately invested in the construction of roads in (politically determined) food production areas. He set up Imo University in a temporary campus at Madonna College Mbano and dilly dallied while looking for land in Obowo, his home local government, for the establishment of the permanent site of the University until Colonel Ike Nwachukwu came in 1983 and sited the institution amidst the gully erosions of Uturu where he spent more money on erosion control than on physical infrastructure. Governor Ike Nwachukwu had the distinction of selling off practically all the major industries established by Governor Mbakwe's administration. But he was a good and fair-minded disciplined soldier. Mbakwe built a wonderful network of major and rural roads all over the state and practically in every constituency. He built the Concord Hotel (today decrepit and a shadow of itself). He launched the construction of Imo Airport. He sanitized the State Education system based on the report of the Education Commission chaired by Dr. S. Okechukwu Mezu that created also the Zonal Education Board Administrative system for Secondary Schools and Local Education Board in each local government to manage elementary schools, a program copied nationwide by other states in the Federation and still in operation in Imo State today. The Commission also abolished school fees and all levies and students only paid a minimal mandatory Registration fee each year for documentation purposes. The Commission also created a 2% Education funding tax on every contract awarded in Imo State to help fund the free education.

    Mbakwe borrowed heavily externally and left his successors massive external loans. The Federal Government debited at source the servicing of these external loans as they became due short-charging successive governments. But Mbakwe's government set up the Okigwe, Owerri and Orlu water schemes, the expansion of Golden Guinea Industries in Umuahia, the Glass Industry in Aba. He set up the Independent Power Source at Amaraku and reticulated both water and electricity supply to practically every constituency in Imo State except in a place like Imerienwe, Ngor Okpala, where he pulled the Electric Polls already supplied to the community as punishment to the community for voting for their son Dr. Nnanna Ukaegbu who contested the governorship election under GNPP against him. Mbakwe's government set up Cardboard Packaging Industry at Owerre-Ebiri, Aluminum Extrusion Industry in Inyishi in Ikeduru, Paint Industry in Mbaise, Bicycle Assembly Plant in Naze, Burnt Brick Industry in Ezinachi and many others including Avutu Poultry Industry in Avutu, Obowo that was supplying poultry and eggs to as far away as Lagos. Imo Newspapers under the Chairmanship of Dr. S. Okechukwu Mezu attained a daily circulation of 150,000. Imo Broadcasting Corporation had a strong radio voice and Imo Television competed strongly with the Nigerian Television Aauthority (NTA) at Aba. Mbakwe's government refurbished the Oguta Motel, the Catering Rest Houses renamed Imo Hotels at Owerri, Aba, Orlu, Okigwe and Umuahia.

The economy of the state was buoyant, construction work was going on every where and in every local government as the Nigerian Peoples Party (NPP) government led by Mbakwe competed ceaselessly with the activities of the Federal Government under the National Party of Nigeria (NPN) Presidential Liaison Officer (PLO) Mr. Collins Obi former Managing Director of African Continental Bank who used the Imo River Basin Authority to create jobs and check erosion in the state. The strides in Imo State, educationally, economically, industrially and socially were phenomenal and yet the entire state revenue and allocation annually then was less than what some Local Governments in Imo State receive monthly today. Governor Mbakwe was not perfect and some of his Commissioners were guilty of corruption, but venial sins compared with the exponential, murderous, criminal and brazen looting of the State Treasury today by Legislators (Legislooters) and the Executive (Executionists).

But who is the greatest Governor of Igbo origin, Samuel Mbakwe or Dr. Michael Okpara? Governor Mbakwe I know very well and very intimately. We share the same initials SOM and worked together night and day during the campaign for his election as Governor of Imo State in 1979. For his second term, I did not vote for him and three months later he was sent to jail by Generals Buhari and Idiagbon. Dr. Michael Okpara, I know fairly well and worked very closely and intimately with him when I was General Ojukwu's and Biafra's Ambassador to Cote d'Ivoire in 1968. Dr. Michael Okpara, Dr. Kenneth Dike, Sir Louis Mbanefo and I cried together at Hotel Ivoire, Abidjan, Room 310 over the Biafran war in 1968 when Owerri fell to the Nigerian soldiers. But in 1979 as Chairman of Golden Guinea, I fired the General Manager, Mr. Iheukwumere, who was Dr. Okpara's relation and who had been there since 1960. Dr. Michael Okpara and Chief Samuel Mbakwe were great courageous and fearless leaders more so than Dr. Nnamdi Azikiwe, a superb intellectual with an encyclopedic memory but ever willing to compromise and Fabian in his philosophy. They all, like all of us, had their faults and Achilles hills. It is like asking, who is the greatest Pope in recent Catholic Church History, Pope Pius X or John Paul II. They were two great Popes. And who is the greatest Nigerian writer, Chinua Achebe or Wole Soyinka. They are both great writers, though personally, I would choose Achebe any day over Soyinka. We are still too close to recent history. Until the generals and associates of Mbakwe and Okpara spill their beans like General Babaginda and General Obasanjo, it is difficult to tell, for between reality and perception, there is always a little gully.

Dr. S. Okechukwu Mezu August 22, 2011

CHAPTER 3
Dr. Nnamdi Azikiwe in Nigerian Politics

(Being Dr. S. Okechukwu Mezu's response to a question from Igboville group on Nnamdi Azikiwe and the Biafran War. Written on November 16, 2011 (Birthday of Dr. Nnamdi Azikiwe).

Who really is Dr. Nnamdi Azikiwe? Once or twice in a century, nature or the Good Lord sends to a people a phenomenon. Dr. Nnamdi Azikiwe, Zik of Africa, was such a phenomenon. He was not just an Igbo man, he was a Nigerian, an African, a Pan-African and a black man. He was a man of great intelligence who valued education and founded the University of Nigeria at Nsukka the progenitor of all universities in Nigeria. Before that, University College Ibadan (UCI) was affiliated with the University of London which also superintended their degrees. Dr. Azikiwe (an Honorary doctorate holder) attended Howard University (Washington, D.C.) and Lincoln University (Lincoln University, Pennsylvania). He earned a Law Degree like myself by correspondence from La Salle Extension University Law School, Chicago. Till today, he is still cherished at Lincoln University and he opened the door to many an African student. In 1998, Lincoln University, under President Niara Sudakasa, organized a symposium in honor of Dr. Azikiwe. It was attended by quite a galaxy of personalities including Dr. Julius Nyerere. My wife and I were at the conference.

Who really is Dr. Nnamdi Azikiwe? In 1970, I edited a book with Dr. Ram Desai entitled, *Black Leaders of the Centuries* (301 p.). It was not an encyclopedia of black leaders. "*The approach , in fact, is analytical rather than encyclopedic. Of primary concern was to identify those leaders (and several they were, are and will be) whose actions, and more important than actions, ideas and ideals have moved the centuries and hanged or influenced the destiny of the black world; to identi-*

Nigeria Ojukwu Azikiwe Biafra Beyond the Rising Sun

fy those leaders whose philosophies, have gone beyond their countries, continents, islands; beyond their immediate geographical location and/or confinement and have caused a change of mind, a change of heart or even orientation amongst black people elsewhere and even the world at large."

These identified leaders included Edward Wilmot Blyden, a pioneer West African Nationalist, William E. B. Du Bois, a Scientist and Public Figure, Booker T. Washington (maligned by many but contributed immensely to the education of the Negro), Marcus Garvey and his brand of African Nationalism, Blaise Diagne and Lamine Gueye from Francophone Africa, Jean Price-Mars, the Father of Haitianism, Nnamdi Azikiwe, a Philosopher and a Man of Ideas, Kwame Nkrumah, a Leninist Czar (in the eyes of Ali Mazrui) Frantz Fanon, (symbolizing the myth and reality of the Negro), Malcolm X (who lived in the age of guns and rhetoric) and Martin Luther King, Jr. (the dreamer who had a vision).

Dr. Nnamdi Azikiwe was a Pan-African Leader who happened to be Igbo. He has no *compere* in Africa, black or brown. Dr. Nnamdi Azikiwe was a rational intellectual leader, the type Nigeria has not seen before and may never see again given the existential situation of today. With patience and equanimity, he sacrificed personal ambition and opportunism and peacefully, peacefully led Nigeria to independence coaxing the tardy North of Sir Ahmadu Bello and restraining the impatient West of Chief Obafemi Awolowo. A more peaceful transition there never was in the continent of Africa or in the history of colonial transfer of power. The chief architect, Dr. Azikiwe, was prepared to play second fiddle to less educated, less experienced, lesser known individuals for the sake of peace, unity and tranquility in Nigeria. His goal, like our own aspirations, was the unity of Africa and the communality of the black world.

For a Pan-Africanist like Dr. Azikiwe (as it was for some of us), the disaggregation of the Luggard Nigerian conglomeration (legitimately or illegitimately conceived) was antithetical to all he fought for and lived for all his life. When Dr. Azikiwe found himself in the Biafran enclave, when the fever of war reached uncontrollable degrees, and dissent was tantamount to insurrection and treasonable felony, a crime against the state, Fabian and pragmatic in his philosophy and conscious of the fact that he who fights and runs away lives to fight another day, suspect to the regime and sidelined because of that, Dr. Nnamdi Azikiwe wrote the Biafran National Anthem. When the Biafran Government could not make any headway on the international arena, Dr. Azikiwe was called upon (like Dr. Michael Okpara and others) to lead delegations to various African and Caribbean countries to explain the Biafran cause and seek recognition for the new nation. I was then completing my Doctoral dissertation at the Sorbonne, University of Paris on a Johns Hopkins University International Exchange Program at the Fondation des Etats-Unis, Paris (1967). Ambassador Ralph Uwechue and I set up the Biafra Historical Research Center in Paris with Ralph Uwechue as Director and myself as the Deputy Director of the pseudo Biafran Office/Embassy. My schedule of duty, amongst other things, included picking up from the airport arriving Biafran dignitaries. Then twenty-seven years old, I was also responsible for their security - Dr. Nnamdi Azikiwe, Dr. Michael Okpara, Prof. Kenneth Dike, Chief C. C. Mojekwu, Chief M. T. Mbu, Air Force Officer Chudi Sokei (killed during the war), Sir Louis Mbanefo, Sonny Odogwu, Dr. Pius Okigbo, George Kurubo (who later defected to Nigeria) etc. - a great responsibility for sometimes five or more of these precious dignitaries had to squeeze into my then brand new Sports Car - Simca Mille Berton - bought March, 1967 with my graduate scholarship and fellowship stipends from the Federal Government of Nigeria, Graduate Fellowship from UNESCO and The Johns Hopkins University

Graduate Felllowship. To paraphrase General Gowon, money then was no problem for me, the problem was how to spend it. That Simca is still preserved till today as a relic of the Biafran War.

One evening in 1968, Dr. Nnamdi Azikiwe had arrived in Paris and I lodged him at the Hotel Napoleon Paris, 40 Avenue de Friedland, 75008 Paris, France a stone throw from the Etoile. I promised him, I would be back by 8:00 p.m. to take him out to dinner and a movie. I was there promptly at eight. I walked into his hotel room. He was sitting on the bed and putting on his socks. I still do not remember how the conversation started. But when I looked at my watch, it was 4:00 a.m. in the morning. I wish, I wish, I wish I had taped the conversation - a detailed course on the beginnings of Nigerian Politics, the journey to independence, the Foster-Sutton Tribunal, an attempt to nail him and imprison him over the African Continental Bank, how the Igbos rallied and overnight recopied volumes and volumes and volumes of African Continental Bank (ACB) bank ledgers, rubbing the new books with soot mixed with palm oil to age and validate. He spoke about the constitutional conferences, his time as Leader of Opposition in Western Nigeria, Premier of Eastern Nigeria, the chance to team up with Chief Awolowo and become Executive Head of Government of Nigeria, the decision to rather save the Nigerian Federation by aligning with Nigerian Peoples Congress (NPC) to become a ceremonial Governor General of the Federation yielding the Prime Ministerial executive post to a school Headmaster Sir Tafawa Balewa to ensure the British granted Nigeria Independence on October 1, 1960 and finally the bombshell - the Biafra War of Independence (Secession). *"When under a military regime and the soldier points a Gun at you,"* ended Dr. Nnamdi Azikiwe, *"you raise up your hand in submission and say 'Yes Sir!'"* *"But then,"* he continued *"when you are out of the range of his gun or he drops his gun under a civilian regime, you leisurely roll up your flowing Agbada,* (one thousand five hundred style) *first with the left hand, then with the right hand and ask him - Gbo Di Anyi - what was it you were saying yesterday?"*

Dr. Nnamdi Azikiwe despite the strong reservations he had about the Ojukwu's declaration of the independence of Biafra, worked with his heart and soul to seek recognition for the new regime and to save the Igbos. The National Council of Nigerian Citizens (NCNC) formerly called [National Council of Nigeria and the Cameroons before Southern Cameroon seceded from Nigeria] under Dr. Nnamdi Azikiwe and after him, Dr. Michael Okpara funded the independence movement in Nyerere's Tanzania and Kaunda's Zambia.

At the risk of digression, it should be mentioned that with the collapse of the League of Nations in 1946 and the rise of the United Nations, mandate territories under the League of Nations became Trust Territories and Southern or British Cameroon two provinces (Bamenda with capital at Bamenda and Southern Cameroon with capital at Buea) on December 6, 1946 was handed over to Great Britain. The Ibadan General Conference of 1950 in Nigeria granted more powers to the Regions in Nigeria and Cameroons elected thirteen Parliamentarians to the Eastern Nigeria House of Assembly with Dr. Endeley as the leader. The London Conference from July 30 to August 22, 1953 created a separate region for Southern Cameroons with capital at Buea and with Dr. E. M. L. Endeley (NCNC) as Premier. Later a February 1959 election led to the defeat of Endeley by the Cameroon nationalist Jon Ngu Foncha and prepared the way, following UN plebiscite on February 11, 1961, for Southern Cameroon joining the rest of French Cameroon while Northern British Cameroon opted to stay with Northern Nigeria. It was a big blow to Nigeria and to NCNC in particular.

I still remember with fondness and exhilaration the NCNC (Azikiwe) and Action Group (Awolowo) campaign in Abak near

Uyo during the 1959 election campaign. I was then one of the twelve pioneer students of Holy Family College Higher School, Abak (a two year Classics College) preparing students for advanced University entrance. Some of the students then included Martin Elechi, present Governor of Ebonyi State and the late Most Rev. Ephraim S. Obot, Catholic Bishop of Idah Diocese, a man of deep faith and humility. Not much has changed really in Nigerian politics as even then at the age of eighteen I viewed their promises then, unfortunately, with a certain tinge of cynicism as illustrated in this poem I wrote, "1959", published in *The Tropical Dawn* [S. Okechukwu Mezu, Black Academy Press, 1970]. Those were the days of classic education with Shakespearean sonnets and iambic pentameter in poetry as prose was reserved for the lower class. The cock was the symbol of NCNC while the palm was the symbol of Action Group :

1959

Vote for cock; vote for the palm
It is the palm that feeds the cock
Ay! it is the cock that sounds the alarm
revealing the crimes that shock

Like kites they droop into a hall
And comfort Uyo for suffering in vain
While Oyo grows like a budding fern
More you will win by heding our call

Schools will floow jobs, water light
Incomes will rise but taxes will be slight
They promise heaven hell and earth
Trust them too for allthey are worth

We shall make villages look like cities
To the city, a country flavor and riches

Enough for the digression. Zambia and Tanzania were conscious of the role Nnamdi Azikiwe and Michael Okpara played in their securing independence. They wanted to stop the suffering and pogrom in Biafra but were reluctant to recognize Biafra until they personally saw Dr. Azikiwe and confirmed where he stood on the issue of independence and secession. General Ojukwu had no alternative but to allow Dr. Azikiwe travel out of Biafra. Dr. Azikiwe obliged and traveled to East Africa through Paris. He also visited President Bourguiba of Tunisia who though supportive could not recognize Biafra because of the dominant Moslem population in Tunisia. This was also the case with President Leopold Sedar Senghor when Dr. Kenneth Dike and I visited him in Dakar in the middle of the Students Riot [*manifestations estudiantines*]. He was exceptionally sympathetic and was prepared to recognize Biafra but even though a Catholic, he (from the minority Serere tribe) was fearful of the reaction of his dominant Moslem population. The airport was cut off from the city and Leopold Senghor had to call in a detachment of French troops with armoured vehicles to ferry us from his personal guest house to the airport where Professor Dike and I stayed with French citizens waiting for the first flight back to Abidjan. On my book on him [*Leopold Sédar Senghor et la défense et illustration de la civilisation noire*, S. Okechukwu Mezu. Paris, Marcel Didier, 1968, 232p.], Senghor had this to say: "You have read everything that I have written. It is the most accurate and comprehensive work on me even though I do not completely agree with some of your conclusions"]. Dr. Nnamdi Azikiwe eventually obtained recognition for Biafra from the two countries, Tanzania and Zambia.

In the case of President Kaunda, Dr. Azikiwe would tell us later, he, Dr. Azikiwe, rubbed Mentholatum on both eyes just

Nigeria Ojukwu Azikiwe Biafra Beyond the Rising Sun [33]

before he entered the room to meet President Kaunda. As Dr. Azikiwe tried to narrate the suffering and pogrom in Biafra, tears profusely and freely flowed from his eyes. President Kenneth Kaunda burst into tears himself and stopped him immediately. "My Master, what do you want?" he said. "Recognition of Biafra," said Nnamdi Azikiwe. "It is done, you have it," said President Kaunda who gave him a handkerchief to clean his teary eyes. Dr. Azikiwe was personally responsible for at least two (Tanzania and Zambia) and possibly three (Hait)i out of the five countries that recognized Biafra.The other two were Cote d'Ivoire and Gabon.

Incidentally, tears worked wonders during the Biafran war. In Paris, President Houphouet Boigny (1905 – 1993), a great and loving friend of Biafra, was visiting Paris with his very elegant and very beautiful wife Marie-Thérèse Houphouët-Boigny, born 1931 whom he married in 1952. The Husband so loved her he built at Yamoussoukro the largest Cathedral in the world, the Basilica of Our Lady of Peace of Yamoussoukro, at a cost of US$300 million.

By co-incidence, during their visit to Paris, Ralph Uwechue and I had just helped a French team go to Biafra to prepare a one hour program on French TV "Cinq Colonnes à la Une." After watching this program on the suffering of the children of Biafra, Mme Houphouet Boigny cried and cried and refused to eat until the husband President Houphouet Boigny did something about Biafra. The husband obliged and met President General de Gaulle who declared following that meeting that *"Le Biafra a le droit à l'auto-determination."* [Biafra has a right to self-determination]. Once back in Abidjan, President Houphouet-Boigny recognized Biafra and General Ojukwu appointed me Biafra Ambassador to Ivory Coast with concurrent accreditation to West African States (1968).

Finally, Dr. Nnamdi Azikiwe is a leader any tribe, nation, country, continent would cherish to have any day, any time, any generation - a consummate intellectual, a pacifist, a democrat *par excellence*, rational, never impetuous, ever willing to listen to all sides, a man of indefatigable energy. He was seventy-five years old when we (R. B. K. Okafor, Jim Nwobodo, Sam Mbakwe, Chief Adeniran Ogunsanya, Solomon Lar, Paul Unongo, Kobani, M. T. Mbu, myself and a host of others) called upon him in 1979 to lead NPP (Nigerian Peoples Party) as the standard bearer and Presidential Candidate - a party formed and organized by Alhaji Waziri Ibrahim who then renamed his branch of the party GNPP (Greater Nigerian Peoples Party). Dr. Azikiwe was ever ready to campaign from ten in the morning till three A.M. the following day in the service of his people, the Igbos. In one instance, we had a scheduled campaign stop for twelve noon at Abriba. The road was long and the stops were many, and without food, we ended up in Abriba after midnight. It was worth it. The entire town converged at their village square, beautiful city in the middle of no where with electricity everywhere. It was exhilarating, invigorating, satisfying as we witnessed the adulation, the love and respect for the great Zik of Africa, Nnamdi Azikiwe. Chief Ibe Agbai Ota was our host and he and his people outdid themselves. Chief Ibe Agbai Ota faced off with Chief Nnanna Kalu, one of the NPN stalwarts and financiers. It was a battle royal in Abriba. Following that incident and similar rallies in Owerri, Aba, Umuahia, Enugu, etc., we knew, that with Zik on the side of NPP, we would sweep the polls in the states of Imo and Anambra. And so we did. We won more than ninety percent of the seats in the Igbo states. Nnamdi Azikiwe has no equal in Nigerian, in fact, African politics - intelligent, cool, careful, fair, royal, dignified and principled.

Would Dr. Nnamdi Azikiwe have seceded from Nigeria and declared Biafra's Independence if he were in control of the situation. The answer is definitely NO. Would Dr. Azikiwe have worked out an accommodation under the Aburi Accord that projected a Confederation. The answer is definitely YES. General Ojukwu is General Ojukwu and Zik of Africa is Zik of Africa and never, never the twain shall meet. The above is a veiled and indirect response to the entreaty from John Okiyi viz: "*I will write Dr. Mezu to weigh in and give us his honest view* [about Dr. Azikiwe and General Ojukwu]. *Our elders are still alive and can guide us."* There will be time to talk about Ojukwu, the war and Ojukwu's return to Nigeria. I was privileged to hold a private and extended discussion with him after his return from exile. It would be inappropriate to delve into those discussions at this time. Following the end of the Biafran War, to detoxify myself and recover my sanity, I had to write about Biafra to get it out of my system. That was the origin of the novel, [Mezu, Sebastian Okechukwu. *Behind the Rising Sun*. (a historical nove about the Biafran war) London, Heinemann, 1971]. Dr. Nnamdi Azikiwe wrote me in 1973 folowing the publication of the novel and considered it the most accurate and comprehensive depiction of the events and the climate during the war. For the *The Times Literary Supplement,* it was "...the most substantial work of fiction yet produced by the war."

CHAPTER 4
CHUKWUEMEKA ODUMEGWU OJUKWU
IN NIGERIAN POLITICS

Chukwuemeka Odumegwu Ojukwu has today become synonymous with Biafra. This was not always the case. He was born in 1933 by Sir Louis Philippe Odumegwu Ojukwu (1909-1966). There is no way one can tell the story of Chukwuemeka Ojukwu without reference to his father whose name as we grew up then in Eastern Nigeria was synonymous with wealth, affluence, success, business acumen. His father did not flaunt his wealth and never used it to destroy anyone. He hails from the Ojukwu's family of Nwakanwa Quarters of Obiuno, Umudim in Nnewi, then in Onitsha Province of Eastern Nigeria. Pa Ojukwu attended primary school in Asaba and later Hope Waddell Training Institute in Duke Town Calabar. After working in the Department of Agriculture, Louis Odumegwu Ojukwu became a Tyre sales clerk with John Holt (Nigeria) Limited. This led him to the establishment of Ojukwu Transport Company which served Eastern Nigerian traders plying the Onitsha-Lagos route at a time Armels Transport Company Limited was not only the only means of public road transport but the post office mail carrier for the region. Then (up to 1961) there was no bridge on the River Niger at Onitsha. A journey from Port-Harcourt to Lagos was a thirty-six hour trip with a stop at Onitsha, disembarkment, a long long wait, then a crossing by ferry or pontoon for the lorry and passengers to Asaba and then re-embarkment on the tedious journey to Ikorodu via Agbanikaka and Ore. Louis Ojukwu gradually organized the largest road haulage company in Nigeria, a veritable empire.

Louis Odumegwu Ojukwu, the business magnate

It was at this juncture that Chukwuemeka Odumegwu Ojukwu was born on November 4, 1933 in Zungeru in Northern

ern Nigeria. Chukwuemeka Ojukwu's mother became estranged with the father. The maternal care that Ojukwu lacked was compensated for by the Father's commendable effort to give his son the best of education, enrolling him at St. Patrick's Primary School, Idumagbo, Lagos, later at the Church Missionary Grammar School (CMS) settling him in the secondary school at King's College, Lagos. By the time Chukwuemeka Ojukwu was 12 years old (1946), his father got him admitted at Epsom College (County of Surrey) in England under the tutelage and guardianship of one his business partners Mr. Constain.

Following the end of World War II, Louis Ojukwu's entrepreneurial spirit converged with the economic boom of the period, the rise of West African Railway Company, the establishment of produce boards (palm oil, palm kernel, etc.) Louis Ojukwu's fleet of vehicles - Ojukwu Transport Company - was there to provide the services for the public and private sectors of the booming economy. He continued to build on his success buying industries, investing in real estate. In the 1950s, he not only invested in many blue chip companies, he became a Director in several of them including Nigerian National Shipping Line, Nigerian Coal Corporation, Shell D'Archy (then headquartered in Shell Camp, Owerri) and African Continental Bank. Eventually he became the first President of the Nigerian Stock Exchange which he led with probity and equanimity. Listed in those days were companies like UAC, Guinness, John Holt, Nigercem and Costain West Africa which was incorporated in 1948 and took over the engineering division of John Holt and Company. Louis Odumegwu Ojukwu incidentally provided his Rolls Royce and his personal driver Mr. Abiefo as chauffeur for Queen Elizabeth when she visited Nigeria in 1956. Little wonder that he was knighted by the Queen of England - Sir Louis Philippe Odumegwu Ojukwu, KBE. He won a seat as a Parliamentarian during Nigeria's First Republic. This is the father of Chukwuemeka Odumegwu Ojukwu, a son, who accepted all the father could give (including a sports car while a student in England) but decided to cut a niche of his own, an Oedipus without its fatal complications. In England, Chukwuemeka Ojukwu had an MG sports car and seemed attracted to the theories of power and governance advocated by Machiavelli *(the Prince)* and Hobbes *(Leviathan)*, as lived by Louis XIV of France and as played or displayed in Shakespeare's *Hamlet*.

Chukwuemeka Odumegwu Ojukwu

After Chukwuemeka Ojukwu at age 22 obtained his Masters (MA) degree, his father had expected him to help run his business empire. History has it that his father prepared for him a well-furnished office and hoped that his young son would help run his prosperous business. Ojukwu's story reads like that of St. Francis de Sales who was destined by his father to be a lawyer so that the young man could eventually take his Father's place as a French Senator from the province of Savoy. For this reason Francis was sent to Padua to study law. After receiving his doctorate, he returned home and, in due time, told his parents he wished to enter the priesthood. His father strongly opposed Francis in this, and only after much patient persuasiveness on the part of the gentle Francis did his father finally consent. There is no room in the psychology of Chukwuemeka Chukwu for patient persuasion or consideration for his father's wishes.

The near-stubborn and highly independent-minded son, Chukwuemeka had other ideas as he joined the Public Service of Eastern Nigeria as an Assistant District Officer (ADO) at Udi near Enugu, capital of Eastern Nigeria. Between 1955 and 1957, he would be posted to Umuahia and Aba also in Eastern Nigeria. What he did next could have triggered a heart attack in another father who did not have the solid frame of mind and body of Sir Louis Philippe Odumegwu Ojukwu. Searching for something he did not know or propelled by forces beyond his control or understanding, Chukwuemeka Ojukwu's stint in administration was short-lived for in 1957, the restless young man joined the British Royal West African Frontier Force (RWAFF) comprising recruits from the then British colonies of Nigeria, Ghana (then Gold Coast), Gambia and Sierra Leone. It was Gen. Adeyinka Adebayo (rtd), a former governor of the defunct Western Region that gave an insight into how Chukwuemeka Ojukwu came to join the Nigerian Army in 1957. Adeyinka Adebayo was the first Nigerian Aide de Camp (ADC) to the then Governor General of Nigeria Sir James Robertson. There was a cocktail party in Umuahia in honor of the Governor General who was represented during the event by the Deputy Governor General Sir Ralph James. Chukwuemeka Ojukwu was then the Assistant District Officer in Umuahia. Eastern Nigeria. Adeyinka Adebayo claims that he had a long discussion with Chukwuemeka Ojukwu and encouraged Ojukwu to join the Nigerian Army. Chukwuemeka Ojukwu eventually did join the Nigerian Army as a cadet. He was sent to Teshie, Ghana and before long to Eaton Hall, England to the Officer Cadet School from where he was affected to the Infantry School at Warminster and later the Small Arms School at Hythe and Joint Services Staff College at Latimer.

When eventually he came back to Nigeria, as one of the most educated officers in the then Nigerian Army, he briefly served with the First Battalion in Kano before being appointed (1958-60) as an Instructor at the Royal West African Frontier Forces Training School in Teshie Ghana from where he had started. Following the independence of Nigeria in October 1960, Chukwuemeka Ojukwu, now a Captain in the Army, became a Staff Officer in the "A" Branch at the Nigerian Army Headquarters in Lagos. His promotion as a Major the same year earned the respect of his father Sir Louis Ojukwu. This singular achievement removed the vista of rebellion and prodigality, and the two (Father and Son) fortunately became reconciled again. Chukwuemeka Ojukwu as a Staff Officer, moved shortly with the First Brigade to Kaduna and from there joined Nigeria's United Nations Peace Keeping Forces in the Congo-Kinshasa in 1962. Following his return to Nigeria, he became the Commander of the Nigerian Fifth Battalion in Kano from 1964 to 1966.

In 1962, Chukwuemeka Ojukwu married his first wife, Njideka Onyekwelu, a Law student he met at Oxford and a native of Awka, Eastern Nigeria, capital now of today's Anambra State. Their first son, Chukwuemeka was born in March 1965. Njideka died in 2010. Chukwuemeka Ojukwu eventually would marry other wives. He had three wives including Stella Onyeador, his second wife who died in 2009. In 1994 Chukwuemeka Ojukwu would marry his third wife, Bianca Onoh, a daughter of Chief C. C. Onoh, a former Governor of Anambra State. Bianca Onoh was Nigeria's Most Beautiful Girl in a 1988 Beauty Pageant. Bianca was then thirty-four years younger than Chukwuemeka Ojukwu.

15 JANUARY BEFORE AND AFTER

The question often asked is whether Chukwuemeka Ojukwu had ulterior motives in joining the Nigerian Armed Froces. I personally knew other cadets who about the same time joined the Nigerian Army from secondary school, like Patrick Amadi, who later became a Brigadier General in the Biafra Army. This particular friend had absolutely no ulterior motive when he joined the armed forces from Holy Ghost College, Owerri. The Army they joined then was actually, The Royal West African Frontier Force. Even then following Nigeria's Independence, the Nigerian Army was commanded by British Officers, the last of whom was Major-General Sir Christopher Welby-Everard (1909 - 1996), the last British army officer to command the Nigerian army (1962-1965).

Generally other Nigerian Army officers were suspicious of the intentions of Chukwuemeka Ojukwu and the other university graduates in their midst. The six graduates then (around January 1966) in the Nigerian Army - Ojukwu, Olutoye, Banjo, Ademoyega, Ifeajuna, and Rotimi - appeared to see themselves as a special class and breed. Adewale Ademoyega was a History graduate of the University of London before joining the Nigerian Army. He and Chukwuemeka Odumegwu Ojukwu were among the first graduates to enrol as officers in the Nigerian Army. Ifeajuna graduated in History from the University of Ibadan. Others were Victor Banjo, Olufemi Olutoye, Adewale Ademoyega, Emmanuel Ifeajuna, and Oluwole Rotimi. Adewale Ademoyega was one of the last graduates to be commissioned directly into the Nigerian Army Infantry. Was it also a coincidence that these officers were in one way or the other involved in the events that led to the first coup d'etat in Nigeria on January 15, 1966 and in the civil war after. It was probably also the internal suspicion within this group of graduates and unwillingness to accept one of them as leader of all that led to the eventual failure of the January 15, 1966 coup d'etat, the failure of the Biafra invasion of the Mid Western Nigeria that opened the flank for the eventual collapse of the Republic of Biafra. Apart from Chukwuma Nzeogwu, a first class disciplined professional soldier who incidentally was not one of the graduate officers, none of the others appeared willing to serve under the other or take command from an equal or a junior officer. It was also Chukwuemeka's justified unwillingness to take command from, or carry out instructions coming from Gowon (who broke the chain of command) that turned a national challenge into an inter-personal conflict between a bruised ego (Gowon) and an unyielding superego (Ojukwu). The rest is history.

All that we know is that Chukwuemeka Ojukwu was not part of the officers that planned the January 15, 1966 coup d'etat. The sub-title above was the title of one of the publications issued by Biafra on the events around the coup d'etat of January 15, 1966 (which I had translated into French during the war as *15 Janvier, Avant et Apres"* while in Paris) and contains a detailed account of the events around that period. There is no need to go through those here again. Together with other books which emanated from Biafra and which I translated then into French for distribution in the Francophone world - *Le probleme de l'unite du Nigeria: Le Cas du Nigeria Oriental*, 52 p.; *Pogrom au Nigeria*, 27 p.; *15 Janvier 1966: Avant et Apres*, 86 p.; *Nigeria et Biafra: Au carrefour des options*, 76 p.; *Allocution devant l'Assemblée Consultative du Nigeria Oriental*, 30 p.; *Proclamation de la Republique du Biafra*, 16 p.; *Allocution lors de la réunion du comité consultatif de l'Organisation de l'Unité Africaine à Addis Abeba, 1968,* 40 p. - they present an overview at least from the Biafra perspective of what happened before, during and after January 15, 1966.

It is not absolutely clear how many Majors were involved in that coup d'etat. The prominent actors included Patrick Chukwuma Kaduna Nzeogwu, Emmanuel Arinze Ifeajuna, Captain Ben Gbulie author of *Nigeria's Five Majors,* Adewale Ademoyega author of *Why We Struck.* (See also *"The Five Majors*: Myth and Reality" by Max Siollun and Obasanjo's *An intimate portrait of Chukwuma Kaduna Nzeogwu).* Other officers that played a role in that overthrow of the government included John Atom Kpera who worked with Nzeogwu. Dan Obi Awuche of the University of Massachussettes, Amherst, MA., USA has compiled a respectable list of creative, historical and supposed eye witness accounts of events. There are also other bibliographies including Aguolu, Christian Chukwunedu. *Nigerian Civil War, 1967-1970; an annotated bibliography,* Boston, G. K. Hall, 1973; Affia, George B. *Nigerian crisis, 1966-1970: a preliminary bibliography.* University of Lagos, Yakubu Gowon Library, 1970; Cervenka, Zdenek. *The Nigerian war, 1967-1970. History of the war: selected bibliography and documents.* Frankfurt am Main, Bernard & Graefe, 1971.

During the January 15, 1966 coup d'etat, Major Nzeogwu maintained that General Ironsi was to have been shot but escaped because he was alerted by a telephone call from Lt. -Col James Pam who was, shortly after that call, abducted and killed. Not only was Prime Minister, Sir Abubakar Tafawa Balewa killed, the Minister of Finance, Festus Okotie-Eboh from the Mid West, the Premier of the Western region, Mr. Samuel Ladoke Akintola, and Brigadier Ademulegun, Colonel Ralph Sodeinde, Brigadier Maimalari and Abogo Largema were also killed. Eventually the Nigerian Army made an offer the surviving Ministers of Abubakar Tafawa Balewa's government could not refuse and they "voluntarily" handed over the Government to the Army and General Aguiyi Ironsi. Faced with bloodshed implicit in a match to Lagos against General Ironsi, Major Chukwumah Nzeogwu and the other coupists - Emmanuel Arinze Ifeajuna, Christian Anuforo, Adewale Ademoyega, Humphrey Chukwuka, Donatus Okafor, Timothy Onwuatuegwu; Captains Ben Gbulie, Emmanuel Nwobosi and Oji - surrendered to Geneeral Ironsi.

The events then in Nigeria had appeared to provide no other exit but a military coup d'etat which was uniformly welcomed by the people very very regretful as the unfortunate and perhaps avoidable death of several political and military leaders was. The fact is that the Nigerian People's Congress of Prime Minister Abubakar Tafawa Balewa had lost control of the government with widespread looting, killing and bombing in the West and Middle Belt sections of Nigeria following the rigged elections and the imprisonment of Chief Obafemi Awolowo who was charged with, and convicted of Treasonably Felony. The Prime Minister, Sir Tafawa Balewa, a gentleman, was even contemplating a state of Emergency. The British Government appears to have known about the planned coup d'etat and according to Victor Adetunji Haffner, in a *Sunday Punch* interview (October 3, 2010), stated that the then British Prime Minister, Harold Wilson, asked Balewa to go with him to Rhodesia (today's Zimbawe) to speak to Ian Smith, the proclaimer of Rhodesia's Unilateral Declaration of Independence but Balewa refused. He also apparently refused the invitation of the British High Commissioner in Lagos to come to his residence on the night of January 14, 1966. Britain did nothing to stop or discourage the contemplated take over of government. We know also that the American Government was aware of the planned *coup d'etat* and even had a detailed and incisively written character analysis of the prime mover, Major Nzeogwu, dated just a week before the *coup d'etat*. The American Government did nothing to stop it. A privately circulated bulletin intercepted by an Igbo nurse in an Atlanta Hospital, provided a succinct character sketch of the smart, efficient, ascetic, non-smoking and celibate Major Nzeogwu. Another similar bulletin would later predict the gory massacres of the Igbos and the end of the regime of General Ironsi in July 1966. In the latter case, I made a desperate attempt (flew from Atlanta to Washington DC) in order to warn, through the Nigerian Embassy, the government of General Ironsi. The Military Attache Colonel Udeh immediately left Washington D.C. for Nigeria with the information. He was in London on his way to Nigeria when the counter coupists struck. He fell short by hours and had to find his way to Eastern Nigeria through Southern Cameroons.

No one knows for certain if the then ceremonial President Dr. Nnamdi Azikiwe was aware of the insinuations of a coup d'etat before he planned his holiday visit to the West Indies handing over power to the President of the Senate, Nwafor Orizu. The revolutionary consciousness then in the army spearheaded by Nzeogwu and the university military recruits once prompted Ironsi to lament: "I asked for soldiers and am being given politicians dressed in uniform." General Ironsi named Lt. Col Ojukwu Military Governor of Eastern Nigeria, Lt. Col. Francis Fajuyi, Military Governor of Western Nigeria, Lt. Col David Ejoor, Military Governor of Mid West and Lt. Col Hassan Katsina as Military Governor of Northern Nigeria.

Once the Army was politicized, ethnic and sectional meaning was read into the January 15 coup d'etat even though the coupists also killed the Igbo Quartermaster-General of the Nigerian Army at Army Headquarters in Lagos, Lt-Col Arthur Unegbe. As pointed out by Nzeogwu, the Northern soldiers that accompanied him during the operation *"had the chance to drop out. More than that, they had bullets. They had been issued with bullets but I was unarmed. If they disagreed they could have shot me....most of the Other Ranks were Northerners but they followed"* (New Nigerian – 18th January 1966).

A retaliation by Northern elements in the Army followed on July 29, 1966 with disastrous consequences leading to the large scale massacre of Igbo and Igbo looking officers including those who defended the nation on January 15, 1966. The coup was led by Murtala Muhammed. Under the command of Major Theophilius Danjuma, the Supreme Commander, General Ironsi was allegedly arrested and subsequently executed by Paiko, William Walbe with Jeremiah Useni driving the truck that drove the General and the Military Governor of Western Nigerian Francis Fajuyi to their execution spot on Iwo Road, Ibadan. Things fell apart and the center could not hold. Yes Chinua Achebe's novel, *A Man of the People*, predicted the military take-over of the government, but the title of his earlier novel *Things Fall Apart* best describes what happened. These events were chronicled in the publication *Pogrom in Nigeria* which I translated into French as *Pogrom au Nigeria*. One thing led to another in a continuing and uncontrollable spiral of events.

THE MAY RIOTS

The May riots followed the declaration of Unitary Form government by General Ironsi. Following General Ironsi's broadcast on Tuesday evening May 24 declaring a unitary government in Nigeria, riots were instigated in Northern Nigeria leading to the killing of more than 600 Igbos in Kano, Bauchi, Sokoto, Katsina, and Zaria with the rioters demanding separation from the rest of Nigeria. Some Igbo traders fought back. But the genie has been let out of the bottle. A cabal led by T/Lt. Col. Murtala Muhammed (Inspector of Signals), T/Major Theophilus Y. Danjuma (General Staff Officer II, SHQ) and Captain Martin Adamu (2nd Battalion, Ikeja) plotted the overthrow of Major General Aguiyi Ironsi. Others involved in the exercise, according to Captain J. N. Garba, included Lt. William Walbe and Lt. Paul Tarfa (Federal Guards), Lts. Muhammadu Buhari and John Longboem (2nd battalion), Lts. Pam Nwatkon (Abeokuta garrison, Recce), Lts Jerry Useni, Ibrahim Bako and Garba Dada (4th battalion, Ibadan), and Lt. Shehu Musa Yar'Adua (Adjutant, 1st battalion, Enugu) and from the Air force Majors Musa Usman and Shittu Alao. Others included Lts. Nuhu Nathan and Malami Nassarawa at Ikeja, IS Umar in Abeokuta, Abdullai Shelleng, Haladu, Magoro, Obeya and Onoja in Ibadan and Captains Jalo and Muhammadu Jega in Enugu. The overthrow and the massacre predicted by the USA came to pass on July 29, 1966.

JULY 29 A MEMORIAL DAY FOR SOME NIGERIANS

July 29, 1966 was a veritable Memorial Day for citizens from Southern Nigeria. The military casualties according to the list provided by the Military Government of Eastern Nigeria included: 33 Eastern, 7 Midwestern, and 3 Western Military Officers and 153 Eastern, 14 Midwestern and 3 Western military men of Other ranks. Of the 33 Eastern officer deaths, there was one Major General, one Lt. Col, nine Majors, eleven Captains, eight Lts. and three 2/Lts. The Midwest lost one Lt. Col, two Majors, two Lts, and two 2/Lts. The West lost one Lt. Col and two 2/Lts. Of the 153 Eastern other ranks who died, eleven were Warrant Officers, twelve Staff Sergeants, thirty Sergeants, twenty five Corporals, twenty-two Lance Corporals and fifty three Privates. The Midwest lost one Warrant Officer, six Staff Sergeants, four Sergeants, two Corporals, and one Lance Corporal. The West lost one Warrant Officer and two Staff Sergeants making for a total of 213 casualties [Eastern Regional Government. *January 15: Before and After.* No. WT/1003/3674/40,000, 1967.]

The list included the following: Major Gen. J.T.U. Aguiyi-lronsi, Lt. Col. F.A. Fajuyi, Lt. Col. I.C. Okoro, T/Lt Col G. Okonweze, Major Christian Anuforo, Major Donatus O. Okafor, Major T.E. Nzegwu (NAF), Major J.K. Obienu, Major Ibanga Ekanem, Major P.C. Obi (NAF), T/Major C.C. Emelifonwu, T/Major B. Nnamani, T /Major J.O.C. Ihedigbo, T/Major O.U. Isong, T/Major A. Drummond, T/Major A.D. Ogunro, Capt. J.I. Chukwueke, Capt. H.A. Iloputaife, Capt. A.O. Akpet, Capt. S.E. Maduabum, Capt. G.N.E. Ugoala, T/Capt P.C. Okoye, T/Capt. I.U. Idika, T/Capt. L.C. Dilibe, T/Capt. J.U. Egere, T/Capt. T.O. Iweanaya, T/Capt. H.A. Auna, T/Capt. R.I. Agbazue, Lt. G. Mbabie, Lt. S.E. Idowu, Lt. E.C.N. Achebe, Lt. S.A. Mbadiwe, Lt. F.P. Jasper, Lt. P.D. Ekedingyo, Lt. S.E. Onwuke, Lt. J.D. Ovuezurie, Lt. A.D.C. Egbuna, Lt. E.B. Orok, Lt. J.U. Ugbe, Lt. Francis Musa, 2/Lt A.O. Olaniyan, 2/Lt. A.R.O. Kasaba, 2/Lt. F.M. Agronaye, 2/Lt. P.K. Onyeneho. The Nigerian Nation at that point had reached a breaking point.

GENERAL GOWON AND GENERAL OJUKWU

The following two broadcasts, more than any other writing or document reveal the personalities of the two war Generals (Gowon and Ojukwu) who would eventaully determine the destiny of Nigeria and Biafra. In his speech to the nation on August 1, 1966 Gowon said among other things:

"This is Lt. Col. Y. Gowon, Army Chief of Staff, speaking to you......I have been brought to the position today of having to shoulder the great responsibilities of this country and the

armed forces with the consent of the majority of the members of the Supreme Military Council as a result of the unfortunate incident that occurred on the early morning of 29 July, 1966....."

As a result of the recent events and the other previous similar ones, I have come to strongly believe that we cannot honestly and sincerely continue in this wise, as the basis of trust and confidence in our unitary system has not been able to stand the test of time. I have already remarked on the issues in question. Suffice to say that, putting all considerations to test - political, economic, as well as social - the base for unity is not there or is so badly rocked, not only once but several times. I, therefore, feel that we should review the issue of our national standing and see if we can help stop the country from drifting away into utter destruction...."

All members of the armed forces are requested to keep within their barracks except on essential duties and when ordered from SHQ. Troops must not terrorize the public, as such action will discredit the new National Military Government......"

I promise you that I shall do all I can to return to civil rule as soon as it can be arranged. I also intend to pursue most vigorously the question of the release of political prisoners. Fellow countrymen, give me your support and I shall endeavour to live up to expectations. Thank you."

Shortly thereafter, on the same day, Lt. Col. Ojukwu, Military Governor of Eastern Nigeria responded:

"In the course of this rebellion, I have had discussions with the Chief of Staff, Supreme Headquarters, Brigadier Ogundipe, who as the next most senior officer in the absence of the Supreme Commander, should have assumed command of the Army........."

"During those discussions, it was understood that the only condition on which the rebels would agree to cease fire were:

that the Republic of Nigeria be split into its component parts; and that all southerners in the North be repatriated to the South and that Northerners resident in the South be repatriated to the North......"

.. the brutal, planned annihilation of officers of Eastern Nigerian origin in the last two days has again cast serious doubts as to whether the people of Nigeria, after these cruel and bloody atrocities, can ever sincerely live together as members of the same nation......."

....I have further conveyed to the Chief of Staff, Supreme Headquarters, my fellow military governors and the Chief of Staff, Army Headquarters, my understanding that the only intention of the announcement made by the Chief of Staff, Army Headquarters today is the restoration of peace in the country whilst immediate negotiations are begun to allow the people of Nigeria to determine the form of their future association. Good night and thank you."

The Igbo and Eastern Nigerians exodus from Northern Nigeria began, one of the largest in the history of humankind. As the wounded arrived back and the bodies of the dead arrived in Eastern Nigeria, people were horrified and incensed. He who is rejected by others cannot reject himself or herself. The tremors were felt beyond the confines of Eastern Nigeria. Eastern Nigerians in the diaspora were more affected. Some who could not handle the stress became mentally challenged. Disparate forces controlled Gowon while desperate forces propelled Ojukwu. The loud drums of war were sounding everywhere. *"To keep Nigeria one is a task that must be done,"* said Nigeria. *"No power on earth can subdue Biafra,"* retorted the Igbos. Emotions were uncontrollable. Reason receded into the darkness of the night. Positions became stratified. Counsellors of compromise on both sides (including Dr. Nnamdi Azikiwe) were tagged as "Sabo," a short form for *Saboteur*.

ABURI ACCORD

A desperate effort was eventually attempted at Aburi, Ghana to solve the intricate predicament Nigeria faced. The Aburi meeting was held between January 4-5, 1967 at Peduase Lodge, Ghana brokered very unfortunately by Lt.-General J. A. Ankrah, Chairman of the Ghana National Liberation Council that had also overthrown Dr. Kwame Nkrumah, first civilian President of Ghana former Gold Coast on 24 February 1966. The Aburi Meeting centered on three issues, namely - the re-organisation of the Armed Forces of Nigeria, the conceptualization of a new Constitutional Arrangement and finally the Issue of displaced persons within Nigeria.

The delegates at the Aburi Conference included The Chairman of the Ghana National Liberation Council - Lt.-General J. A. Ankrah as Chairman; Lt.-Col. Yakubu Gowon- Head of State of Nigeria, Lt.-Col. Odumegwu Ojukwu - Governor Eastern Nigeria, Major Mobolaji Johnson, Lt.-Col. Hassan Katsina - Governor of Northern Nigeria, Lt.-Col. David Ejoor, Governor Mid-Western Nigeria, Commodore Joseph Edet Akinwale Wey, Colonel Robert Adebayo, Governor of Western Nigeria, Alhaji Kam Selem and Mr. T. Omo-Bare. Others who attended included: N. Akpan, Secretary to the Military Governor, Eastern Nigeria; Alhaji Ali Akilu, Secretary to the Military Governor, Northern Nigeria, D. Lawani, Under Secretary, Military Governor's Office, Mid-Western Nigeria, P. Odumosu, Secretary to the Military Governor, Western Nigeria, and S. Akenzua, Permanent Under-Secretary, Federal Cabinet Office.

Some of the agreements reached included:

On the implementation of the agreement reached by representatives of the Military Leaders on 9 August, 1966, the Council reaffirmed the principle that Army personnel of Northern origin should return to the North from the West. In order to meet the security needs of the West it was agreed that a crash programme of recruitment and training was necessary but that the details should be examined after the Military Committee had finished its work.

It was in the course of discussing the reorganization of the Army that the crucial issue of the assumption by Lt.-Col. Gowon of the offices of Supreme Commander and Head of the Federal Military Government arose. The Governor of the East, in explaining why it was impossible for him to recognize Lt.-Col. Gowon as Supreme Commander, pointed out that the fate of Major-General Aguiyi-Ironsi, the legitimate Supreme Commander, was yet unknown and so no one could succeed him; that in the absence of Major-General Aguiyi-Ironsi whoever was the next senior officer in rank should manage the affairs of the country; and that the East was never party to any decision to appoint Lt.-Col. Gowon Supreme Commander. Subsequently, Lt.-Col. Gowon volunteered information regarding the murder of the Major General and his host, Lt.-Col. Adekunle Fajuyi, on 29 July, 1966. The Supreme Military Council decided to accord the late military leaders the full honours due to them.

The Supreme Military Council recognized that with the demise of Major-General Aguiyi-Ironsi no other Military Leader could command the support of the entire Nigerian Army and that a new arrangement was necessary for an effective administration of the whole country. The Council also took cognizance of the fact that extreme centralization had been the bane of the Military Regime in the past and that it was essential to re-define the powers of the Federal Military Government vis-a-vis the Regional Military Governments in order to ensure public confidence and co-operation.

Unfortunately, after the Aburi Accord, some Permanent Secretaries in Lagos met and criticized the decisions reached by the Supreme Military Council objecting particularly to the reorganization of the Army and the proposed new title of "Commander-in-Chief" which they saw as a "subtle way of either abolishing the post of Supreme Commander or declaring it vacant to be filled by *unanimous* decision of the Supreme Military Council." They felt also that the Accra decision transfers the Executive Authority of the Federal Military Government from the Head of the Federal Military Government and Supreme Commander (in accordance with Decree No. 1) to the Supreme Military Council with the presumed implication that the Commander-in-Chief would have no power of control or dismissal over the Regional Governors. Following the refusal of Gowon to implement the Aburi Accord, there was no basis of trust left between Ojukwu and Gowon or between Eastern Nigeria and the rest of the Federation of Nigeria. Northern Nigerians saw Aburi as a victory for Eastern Nigeria and the outwitting of Gowon, a simple leader desirous of peace by an Oxford educated and intelligent Ojukwu. Declaration of the indepednece of Biafra was a matter of time. Chief Obafemi Awolowo warned that if Eastern Nigeria seceded that Western Nigeria will secede immediately. He never did. War or what Gowon called a "police action," would follow immediately.

NIGERIAN BIAFRA WAR

Nigeria declared war on Biafra on July 6, 1967. I personally saw and lived the Biafra war in various theaters at home and abroad - in Biafra at Ezeogba Emekuku, Owerri, Mbaise, Umuahia and Uli; abroad in Paris, Lisbon, Gabon, Sau Tome, Abidjan, Niamey, Addis Ababa, Switzerland, Germany, USA, London and Canada. At one point, the Biafra documents I translated into French, were printed in France. I carried the documents in suitcases across the English Channel to London and mailed them from five different post offices back to France and other European capitals to various Embassies and International Agencies in order to evade the then prying eyes of French and Nigerian Security services. It was a joy working then with Raph Uwechue. We basically worked eighteen to twenty hours a day. It was a two-man Embassy with a French Secretary virtually coordinating Biafran activities - military, economic, relief services, publicity, protocol - in Europe and Francophone Africa.

I do not have the heart again to live through what happened in Biafra. My novel, *Behind the Rising Sun,* is there to tell the story. For me it was an cleansing. Let us allow Mr. Maxwell Cohen, Lawyer and member of the International Law Committee of the American Bar Association and adviser to the Biafran Government on the United Nations Genocide Convention to present his eye-witness account entitled "An Eyewitness to Genocide in Biafra," on the occasion of the First International Conference on Biafra in New York on December 7, 1968.

Curiously, in the thousands of books, reports and speeches that I have read relating to the Biafra situation, there has been no reference made to an amazing coincidence of three aspects. I wonder if I could call your attention to this omission, and ask you to consider the significance. (1) I don't know of any other situation in my generation, which has combined in one instance the curious aspects of the great moral verbalization, the greatest example of governmental duplicity, and the magnificent social dynamics of a youthful generation. Let me clarify. The moral tone of this atrocious war, and every war is an atrocity, has been set by students, middle class individuals or families, and certain institutions. The aspect of governmental duplicity has been set by commissions, by Ambassadors, by various governmental functionaries; and the moral dynamic tone has been set by college students in the United States and all over the world. Let me be even more specific before we get into our subject this morning. I have seen in Biafra the extraordinarily courageous activity and conduct of clergymen, of the Catholic faith, of the Protestant faith, or of Welfare Work-

ers of the World Council of Churches and Catholic Service Organizations and B'nai B'rith. I have seen instances where the nobility of humanity reaches such heights as to make you feel and accept the concept of the Divinity. I have seen instances of courage by Priests who remained in hospitals that were bombed, who remained in feeding centers that were subject to bombing, who could have escaped and who remained where they were knowing full well that if they were ever captured the best they could hope for would be as quick a death as possible. I also think, for example, of the tremendously courageous behavior of the Welfare Workers who make these thoroughly dangerous flights into Biafra every single night.

The other side of the coin is the aspect of governmental duplicity. When I was in Biafra September 28th, I was subjected to a bombing in which 74 people were killed, about 200 yards away from me in a market place. Hundreds were shot at, two bombs were dropped, three rockets fired. An Egyptian pilot in a Russian plane strafed a number of kids playing in a field right near the hotel where I was staying. I witnessed it. I saw it. Shrapnel hit an aluminum case ten feet away from me. That evening, I heard a broadcast on BBC. General Alexander assured the world there was no evidence in Biafra of atrocity, no evidence of indiscriminate bombing, no evidence of genocide whatsoever. There have been since that time six different commissions all claiming no evidence of atrocity, of bombing, of genocide. The singular aspect of all these Commissions is the fact that none of them has ever gone into Biafra. Not a single one. How can they discuss the commission of a crime by sitting in the warm corner of the perpetrator of the crime accepting his assurance that the crime has not taken place."

http://www.biafraland.com/genocide_in_biafra_speech.htm

I was also a witness to similar atrocities on the streets of Umuahia and in markets in Ahiara, Mbaise. War is cruel to both sides and innocent Nigerians became victims also to the few air raids the Biafra Air Force was able to muster with devastating precision. Only a nation of fools fights a civil war a second time.

For the first time in Cold War history, Great Britain, the United States and Communist Soviet Union combined together and waged war against a defenseless people who have been victims of genocide. Oil in the Niger Delta area of Biafra was at stake. Starvation was used as a weapon of war. Very few (Easterners and foreigners alike) could look at pictures of Biafra Kwashiokor children, innocent angels and victims of war, rickety skeletons covered with a thin barely visible film of skin beamed to them by the American TV during their dinner.

On January 8, 1970, General Ojukwu took the last plane out of Biafra and into exile in Ivory Coast. His Chief of Staff, Major-General Obong Philip Effiong (1925-2003) took over as Officer Administering the Government of Biafra, declared cease-fire on January 12, 1970 and submitted to the Federal Military Government of Nigeria supported by Brigadier Tony Eze, Brigadier Patrick Amadi, Colonel Joe ("Air Raid") Achuzia and Colonel Patrick Anwuna. Biafra lost over one million people due to the war and starvation. Ojukwu ruled Biafra from May 30, 1967 until January 8, 1970.

Thus came to an end the Republic of Biafra, a hope and dream for many, a nighmare for some and an unwelcome revolutionary enclave for others. Comprised of many ethnic groups who were disrustful of the majority Igbos, it had a population then of over 15 million people in an area of approximately 48,000 square kilometers. Biafra was heavily endowed with human and material resources including palm oil, coal, natural gas, crude oil, timber, lime stone, iron ore and other minerals. It quickly established the University of Biafra with Professor Eni Njoku (formerly Vice Chancellor of the University of Lagos) as the Vice Chancellor and projected a University of Science and Technology at Port-Harcourt with Professor Kenneth Dike (formerly first Vice Chancellor of the University of Ibadan) as the Vice Chancellor.

Before then the Republic of Biafra had been recognized by (a) Tanzania on April 13, 1968 ([Dr. (Mwalimu) Julius Nyerere], (b) Gabon on May 8, 1968 by President Albert Bernard Bongo; (c) Côte d'Ivoire on May 14, 1968 by President Felix Houphöet-Biogny; (d) Zambia on May 20, 1968 by Dr. Kenneth Kaunda; (e) Haiti on March 22, 1969 by Dr. Francois (Papa Doc) Duvalier. The Biafra National Anthem was adapted from a poem written by Dr. Nnamdi Azikiwe who was principally responsible for the recognition of Biafra by President Julius Nyerere and President Kenneth Kaunda. Eventually Dr. Azikiwe left Biafra and declared support for the Military Government of Nigeria. France's General de Gaulle declared that Biafra has a right to self-determination and discretely supported Biafra through President Houphouet-Boigny and Ivory Coast. Portugal was the nerve center of Biafra tele-communications in Europe when the telex was king of written and coded communications. Israel also provided intelligence and military help using Bouake airport in Ivory Coast. I held meetings with the Israeli Foreign Minister Abba Eban in Abidjan, Ivory Coast. Help from Rhodesia and South Africa was minimal. The Vatican City, Ireland through Holy Ghost Fathers, Caritas Internationalis, Terre des Hommes, Medicins sans Frontier, Joint Church Aid, Catholic Relief Services of the United States of America, World Council of Churches (WCC), International Committee of the Red Cross (ICRC), and so many other agencies, helped save millions of Biafrans from starvation and annihilation.

Let us briefly review the lamentations of Titi's mother in the lst chapter of *Behind the Rising Sun*:

"From village to village, they had wandered like a bunch of beggars. There had been no placae to sleep or to lay their heads. As they moved farther and farther away, the sound of shelling had moved closer and closer. Every day, they had that

another village had fallen to the enemy. Every day, they had been joined by new groups of refugees. Every night, they had discovered that they had to run once again from their new place of abode. In the market place, in the home, in the camp, planes had flown over thier heads. The next moment there would be people dead beside them, a house near them levelled.

"War is a hopeless thing," she continued. You can never tell when it will be your turn, when the plane will strike, when it will bomb your house, your office or simply strike you in bed. It is worse than a pest, worse than an epidemic.There used to be vaccines against pests and epidemics. But there is no remedy against the misery and insecurity of war."

BIAFRA NATIONAL ANTHEM
Land of the Rising Sun

Land of the rising sun, we love and cherish,
Beloved homeland of our brave heroes;
We must defend our lives or we shall perish,
We shall protect our hearth from all our foes;
But if the price is death for all we hold dear,
Then let us die without a shred of fear.

Hail to Biafra, consecrated nation,
Oh fatherland, this be our solemn pledge:
Defending thee shall be a dedication,
Spilling our blood we'll count a privilege;
The waving standard which emboldens the free
Shall always be our flag of liberty.

We shall emerge triumphant from this ordeal, And through the crucible unscathed we'll pass; When we are poised the wounds of battle to heal,

We shall remember those who died in mass;
Then shall our trumpets peal the glorious song
Of victory we scored o'er might and wrong.

Oh God, protect us from the hidden pitfall,
Guide all our movements lest we go astray;
Give us the strength to heed the humanist call:
'To give and not to count the cost" each day;
Bless those who rule to serve with resoluteness,
To make this clime a land of righteousness.

Adapted from a poem by Dr. Nnamdi Azikiwe

OFFICERS OF THE REPUBLIC OF BIAFRA

The following were officers of the Republic of Biafra.

Head of State: Gen. Chukwuemeka Odumegwu Ojukwu, jssc.

Chief of General Staff: Major-General Philip Effiong

Chief Secretary: Mr. N. U. Akpan

GOC Biafran Army: Major-General Alexander Madiebo [replaced Brigadier Hilary Njoku]

Commander, Biafran Air Force: Wing Commander G. I. Ezeilo

Commander, Biafran Navy: Captain. W. A. Anuku

Director of Military Intelligence: Mr. Bernard Odogwu

Military Assistant to the C-in-C: Colonel David Ogunewe

Principal Officer to the C-in-C: Colonel Patrick Anwuna

Prominent Division GOCs:
Brigadier Tony Eze, Brigadier Pat Amadi, Colonel Joe ('Air Raid') Achuzie, Colonel Nsudo, Colonel Iheanacho, Colonel Archibong, etc.

GOC, 101 (Republic of Benin Liberation Army):
Brigadier Victor Banjo [later executed for sabotage]

Inspector-General of Police: Mr. P. I. Okeke

Governor Bank of Biafra : Dr. Sylvester Ugoh

Chief Medical Director ; Dr. Simon E. Onwu

Chief Justice: Sir Louis Mbanefo

Attorney-General & Commissioner for Justice:
Mr. J. I. Emembolu

Special Advisers to the Head of State:
Dr. Akanu Ibiam & Dr. M. I. Okpara [respectively former Governor and Premier of defunct Eastern Nigeria]

Biafra's Roving Ambassadors: Dr. Nnamdi Azikiwe, (first President of Nigeria); Dr. Kingsley Ozumba (K. O.) Mbadiwe, Dr. Michael Okpara, Dr. Pius Okigpo, Chief C. C. Mojekwu, Mr. Nwokedi, Chief Justice Louis Mbanefo, Professor Kenneth Onwuka Dike and others.

Chairman , Consultative Assembly: Dr. Alvan Ikoku

Chairman, Atrocities Commission: Mr. G. C. M. Onyiuke

Chairman, Rehabilitation Commission: Dr. S. E. Imoke

Chairman, Development Commission: Professor A. Modebe

Chairman, Marketing Board: Mr. C. C. Mordi

Relief Coordinator: Dr. S. E. Cookey

Chairman, Food Directorate: Mr. Bob Ogbuagu

Chairman, Housing Directorate: Mr. P. O. Nwakoby

Commissioner of Home Affairs: Mr. C. C. Mojekwu

Commissioner for Information: Dr. Ifeagwu Eke

Commissioner for Health: Mr. James Udo-Affiah

Commissioner for Transport & Communication: Mr. Felix Iheanacho

Commissioner for Foreign Affairs: Mr. M. T. Mbu.
Commissioner for Labor: Mr. Emmanuel Aguma

Commissioner for Rural Development: Chief Frank Opigo

Commissioner for Agriculture: Professor Eyo Bassey Ndem

Commissioner for Forestry & Animal Husbandry: Mr. U. O. Imo

Biafra Representative in London: Mr. Ignatius S. Kogbara

Biafra Representative in France: Mr. Ralph Uwechue

Nigeria Ojukwu Azikiwe Biafra Beyond the Rising Sun [61]

Biafra Representative in Cote d'Ivoire:
Dr. S. Okechukwu Mezu

Biafra Representative in Lisbon: Mr. O. U. Ikpa **Biafra**

Representative in Tanzania: Mr Austin Okwu **Biafra**

Representative in New York: Aggrey K. Orji **Ojukwu's**

Biafra Personal Representative in New York
Dr. Lemeh

Biafra Representative in Bonn: Dr. Aaron Ogbonna

Biafra Representative in Canada: Dr. Otue

Biafra Representative in Libreville: Mr. Hyacinth Ugwu

Biafra Representative in Sau Tome: Mr. Egbert Nwogu

Vice-Chancellor, University of Biafra: Professor Eni Njoku [formerly VC, University of Lagos]

Director, War Information Bureau: Dr. Michael C. J. Echeruo
Director Military Aid: Count Carl Gustav von Rosen (a Swede)

Relief Organizations: Caritas Internationalis, World Council of Churches (WCC), International Committee of the Red Cross (ICRC), etc.

Nigeria Declaration of War: July 6, 1967

Military Administrator of Republic of Benin:
Major (Dr.) Albert Okonkwo

Execution of coup plotters in Enugu: September 25, 1967
[Brigadier Victor Banjo, Lt. Colonel Emmanuel Ifeajuna, Major Alale, and Mr. Sam Agbam]

End of War: January 12, 1970

Official Date of Cessation of Hostilities: January 15, 1970

DIVISIONAL ADMINISTRATORS IN THE REPUBLIC OF BIAFRA

Aba	Mr. Moses Onwuma
	later (Lt. Col. Ben Gbulie)
Abakaliki	Mr. Samuel Mgbada
Annang	Chief Ekukinam Bassey
Awka	Mr. Paul Nwokedi
Calabar	Prof. Eyo Bassey Ndem
Degema	Mr. S. N. Dikibo
Eket	Mr. S. J. Edoho
Enugu	Mr. Christian Chukwuma Onoh
Nsukka	Mr. Frank Onyeke
Ogoja	Mr. Frank Ugbut
Oji River	Dr. Godwin A. Odenigwe
Okigwe	Mr. Samuel Onunaka Mbakwe
Onitsha	Mr. R. I. Iweka
Opobo	Dr. S. J. Cookey
Orlu	Mr. R. I. Uzoma
Owerri	Mr. Duke Njiribeakor
Port Harcourt	Mr. Emmanuel Aguma
Umuahia	Mr. Simeon Ojukwu
Uyo	Chief J. Udo-Affiah
Yenegoa	Chief Frank Opigo

Republic of Benin Major Dr. Albert Okonkwo, Military Administrator

OJUKWU IN EXILE

Chukwuemeka Ojukwu spent twelve years in exile in Ivory Coast as guest of President Houphouet Boigny who granted him political asylum. He lived firstly at Yamoussoukoro and later in Abidjan but he kept in touch with developments in Nigeria and took time to study French. Before Ojukwu's exile, I was several times a dinner guest of President Houphouet Boigny at his palace in Yamoussoukoro. Ojukwu returned from exile in 1982.

OJUKWU THE FAMILY MAN

It has been reported that Ojukwu's first married one Elizabeth Okoli from Nnukwu, in Awka town, Anambra State. Elizabeth Okoli was a senior Nursing Sister by profession. The marriage reportedly took place between 1956 and 1958. They had no children. Eventually this daughter of the first Nigerian Post-Master General of Nigeria, following their divorce, married one Dr. Onuorah

Chukwuemeka Ojukwu, then married Njideka his second wife and second daughter of C.T. Onyekwelu of then grammophone record fame from Nawfia, Njikoka Local Government Area of Anambra State. Njideka Onyekwelu was born on December 25, 1933 and died in 2010. Her mother was Mrs. Malinda Nnuaku Onyekwelu. Chukwuemeka Ojukwu and Njideka Onyekwelu had met again in London having been earlier introduced by their parents both outstanding businessmen in Onitsha. After their marriage, she moved from Lagos to Kano in 1965 where her husband was staying. The marriage was celebrated at Apapa, Lagos (1962) with a reception at Sir Odumegwu's Ikoyi residence.

Reportedly, she had been married to Dr. Menz and had two children when they separated and Chukwuemeka Ojukwu then married her and they had three children - Emeka, Mimi and Okigbo. Njideka was the wife of Ojukwu that Biafrans knew and loved during the war. The two were married when Chukwuemeka Ojukwu was the 5th Battalion Commander. She was there when Ojukwu was appointed the Governor of Eastern Nigeria. She was with him during the war. She went into exile with Chukwuemeka Ojukwu to Ivory Coast until Stella Onyeador of Arochukwu came into the scene and Njideka walked out of the marriage and moved to London.

Chukwuemeka Ojukwu would come back from exile in 1982 with Stella Onyeador. They had no children together and the two also separated and Bianca Odinaka Onoh, daughter of former Governor of Anambra State, Chief Christian Chukwuemeka Onoh, came into the scene. It was Bianca Onoh who looked after Chukwuemeka Ojukwu following his stroke in Enugu, in December 2010 until his death in a London Hospital on November 26, 2011.

OJUKWU RETURNS FROM EXILE

Chukwuemeka Odumegwu Ojukwu was pardoned by President Alhaji Shehu Shagari of the National Party of Nigeria (NPN). Ojukwu returned home to Nigeria in 1982 to a tumultous welcome. The Nigerian Peoples Party (NPP)then controlling Imo State and Anambra State tried desperately to recruit him into the NPP. I travelled with Chief Sam Onunaka Mbakwe's cabinet to pay him a courtesy visit in Nnewi. It was a joyful reunion. At the end of the visit, as Governor Mbakwe and his entourage got into his car to leave, Chukwuemeka Ojukwu and I moved aside reminiscened and spoke at length and in confidence in French. One of my final questions to him was why he joined the NPN. Needless to say or rather enough to say that I was very satisfied with his answer. Suffice to say also, because of the confidential nature of our discussions that General Odumegwu Ojukwu was still a Biafran to the core.

THE IRONY OF HISTORY

In an incredible irony of history, on the eve of Chukwuemeka Ojukwu's death, those same loud drums of war were sounding again in Nigeria forty years after the civil war. Nothing had changed; the nation had learned nothing and government as well as governmance had become more problematic. His death coincided with the unleashing of anarchy and brutality that even surpassed the riots in Western Nigeria in 1965 and the pogrom against Eastern Nigerians in Northern Nigeria in 1966. Chukwuemeka Odumegwu Ojukwu was mourned by friends and foes alike - some with sincerity others out of participation mystic. Gen. Mohammadu Buhari had this to say on General Ojukwu's Passing:

It is with great shock that I received the news of the passing away of Dim Chukwuemeka Odumegwu Ojukwu on Saturday morning. Though he had been sick for some time, we were all hoping and praying that we would welcome him back home in good health; but, unfortunately, this was not to be.

I would like to offer my heartfelt condolences to Mrs. Bianca Ojukwu ...and the Ojukwu extended family, the governments of the South-Eastern states, Ndigbo in Nigeria and in the Diaspora, and to the entirety of the people of Nigeria on this great loss. In his life, Dim Ojukwu had been many things to many people—a soldier, a leader, a rebel and a politician. It was in his role as rebel to the nation and a symbol to his people and fighter for their rights that he came to play a pivotal role in the tragic civil war in which we found ourselves in trenches facing each other as brother-enemies fighting to preserve the unity and territorial integrity of our fatherland. Later, we would still be fighting, this time together in the trenches of Nigeria's politics, to finish the battle for unity and progress.

In the course of these years, we came to understand ourselves well and respect each other deeply, as compatriots searching for solutions to the problems confronting our country, as concerned leaders of our respective political groupings; and, in the process, as friends and guests in each other's homes. And in all our transactions and engagements on and off the political scene, I found Dim Ojukwu a most forthright and honourable player. He was a tireless, intelligent, focused and frank negotiator who would never give a word he wouldn't keep.

No doubt, the understanding and trust that developed between us and between him and other political actors contributed in no small measure to the overall success of the process of national integration on the political front. And with his passing away, the nation has lost a leader of great humanity and a political actor of great colour and character and a voice for moderation; and Ndigbo has lost a brave captain who has now passed to the status of a legend.

Dim Ojukwu will be greatly missed. I pray to God to give his family, Ndigbo and the nation the fortitude to bear a loss that can in many ways be said to be truly irreparable."
General Muhammadu Buhari, GCFRS

Eastern Nigerians and the Igbos, in particular, had lost one who symbolized their trials, their struggle, their finest moment. His death did not signal the end of an era but the beginning of one. As he lay even on his death bed, unscrupu;ous poiticians used his name to seek for votes. When he finally died, politicians who did little or nothing to live up to the principles Ojukwu stood for, cried more than the real mourners. Frantic efforts were made to give him a befitting burial by repairing roads to his village. If we valued him that much and he has done so much for us, why did we not give him that honor while he was alive? How soon have we forgotten other Igbo leaders, Nnamdi Azikiwe, Michael Okpara, Samuel Mbakwe, Akanu Ibiam, etc. and have we made any effort to repair those village roads that lead to their homes. They sacrificed their lives to ensure that the future generation had education and good government.

What efforts have we made to even maintain the educational, industrial and agricultural legacies they left behind - Golden Guinea Industires, Premier Breweries, Nkalagu Cement Industry, Asbestos Industries, Glass Industries, Modern Ceramics Industry, Shoe Industry, Adapalm, Cashew Industries, Concorde Hotel, Hotel Presidential, the Universities, the secondary school system, the elementary school system - peace, tranquility and respect for human life, hard work and service to the country and the race. Ralph Uwazurike and the Movement for the Actualization of the Soverign State of Biafra (MASSOB) can and should actualize these principles within the subject states and through the existing structure through interstate cooperation, intrastate economic policies, road and transport development, joint projects in the area of electricity generation and distribution, harmonized technological development and interparliamentary associations.

In a recent interview, following the death of Odumegwu Ojukwu, Ralph Uwazurike had this to say about Ojukwu and Nigeria:

"The masses themselves know who their leaders are and accord them respect and acceptance as Ojukwu was accorded due to his pedigree, his love for his people, the amount of risk he was prepared to take for the Igbo race, the strength he gave to us, the leadership he afforded us ... . Ojukwu has lived his life and we are feeling so much because of his importance to us. He made himself important to us because of his work, otherwise it is not as if people wouldn't die. He lived his normal life, he didn't die by accident, he was not assassinated, so

what we should do is honour him and uphold all those virtues for which he lived and life continues.... A leader should be courageous; he should protect his people by all means, at all costs.... do you know how many people that die as a result of the misrule of our leaders? The roads are not repaired, millions of people die by accident. We have the resources to repair the roads, but instead of repairing the roads, you go to Dubai to buy houses or you go to Swiss Bank and put the money there. Are you helping the masses? Go to hospitals, the drugs are not there." http://chukseoluigbo.blogspot.com/2012/02/ralph-uwazuruike-south-east-governors.html

Let us again hear the words of exhortation of General Chukwuemeka Odumegwu Ojukwu when he articulated the philosophy and principles of the Biafran Revolution *The Ahiara Declaration* (1968) and today he speaks to us from the land beyond:

PROUD AND COURAGEOUS BIAFRANS, FELLOW COUNTRY MEN AND WOMEN

I salute you. Today, as I look back over our two years as a sovereign and independent nation, I am overwhelmed with the feeling of pride and satisfaction in our performance and achievement as a people. Our indomitable will, our courage, our endurance of the severest privations, our resourcefulness and inventiveness in the face of tremendous odds and dangers, have become proverbial in a world so bereft of heroism, and have become a source of frustration to Nigeria and her foreign masters.

For this and for the many miracles of our time, let us give thanks to Almighty God. I congratulate all Biafrans at home and abroad. I thank you all the part you have played and have continued to play in this struggle, for your devotion to the high ideals and principles on which this Republic was founded. I thank you for your absolute commitment to the cause for which our youth are making daily, the supreme sacrifice, and a cause for which we all have been dispossessed, blockaded, bombarded, starved and massacred. I salute you for your tenacity of purpose and amazing steadfastness under siege.

I salute the memory of the many patriots who have laid down their lives in defence of our Fatherland. I salute the memory of all Biafrans - men, women and children - who died victims of the Nigerian crime of genocide. We shall never forget them. Please God, their sacrifice shall not be in vain. For the dead on the other side of this conflict, may their souls rest in peace. To our friends and well-wishers, to the growing band of men and women around the world who have, in spite of the vile propaganda mounted against us, identified themselves with the justice of our cause, in particular to our courageous friends, officers and staff of the Relief Agencies and humanitarian organisations, pilots who daily offer themselves in sacrifice that our people might be saved; to Governments, in particular Tanzania, Gabon, Ivory Coast, Zambia and Haiti. I give my warmest thanks and those of our entire people.

Former President of Nigeria General Olusegun Obasanjo expressed an "unrepentant" sadness on the death of Chukwuemeka Ojukwu: "It is with deep sadness that I received the news of the demise of my friend and colleague. He and I were subalterns in the army at Nigeria's independence in 1960. In a way, his death marks the end of an era in Nigeria."

This writer sees Ojukwu's death rather as possibly the beginning of a new era in Nigeria. If he was quoted correctly, General Obasanjo was decidedly wrong when he opined that General Ojukwu discussed with him the "possibility of an expression of remorse from Ojukwu" about the Civil War. It is inconceivable that Odumegwu Ojukwu or Okechukwu Mezu or any other participant in that struggle would consider expressing remorse about a war imposed on Biafrans whose only crime was retreatng to their enclave when pogromized by their "own dear native land." Yes tribe and tongue may differ but Biafrans believed we all in Nigeria stood together in brotherhood. From the grave Chukwuemeka Ojukwu sends a telling reply without equivocation to Olusegun Obasanjo: "*Until my last dying breath, I shall continue to think of my Jerusalem, Biafra*" Odumegwu Ojukwu said while he was still alive and breathing. To Nigeria's *No Victor No Vanquished*, Biafrans say *No Apology, No Remorse.*

CHAPTER 5

INHERENT DESIRE TO THWART THE PEOPLE'S MANDATE IN NIGERIA'S POLITICAL HISTORY

Nigeria and the world have watched, with studied silence and stupefaction, the macabre political and electoral dance on a circus trampoline going on in the country. The nation had performed similar dances of death before, from 1963 - 1965, from 1981-1983, from 1991-1993 and now the continuing current dance that started in 2001. The players, many of whom were there as major actors from 1963 through 1970, seem to have learned nothing from history and gained less from experience. Power is transient and corrupting and absolute power not only corrupts absolutely but vanishes like a meteor leaving in its stead disaster and regrets. The same *processus* has started.

Negative Bonds of Union

Our nationalistic leaders and heroes who were united in their fight against the common enemy, colonialism, soon fell apart when the goal of independence appeared to have been achieved and treated each other like villains: Dr. Nnamdi Azikiwe and Mbonu Ojike of the N.C.N.C. (National Council of Nigeria and the Cameroons); Chief Obafemi Awolowo and Chief S. L. Akintola of Nigeria's Action Group (AG); Chief Obafemi Awolowo, Dr. Nnamdi Azikiwe and Sir Ahmadu Bello, joint architects of Nigeria's independence. This phenomenon was not Nigerian alone. It was the same in every country: Kwame Nkrumah and Busia in Ghana; Léopold Senghor and Mamadou Dia in Senegal; Houari Boumedienne and Ahmed ben Bella in Algeria; Milton Obote and the Kabaka of Buganda in Uganda; Jomo Kenyatta and Oginga Odinga in Kenya; Patrice Lumumba and Joseph Kasavubu in Congo (Kinshasa). The list is not meant to be comprehensive or exhaustive. Even within various sections of the same country, and within even political parties, such dissensions often assumed the proportions of mortal rivalry. A power struggle led to the victimization, imprisonment or death of political opponents, in fact, of former political colleagues and even comrades-in-arms.

Government of the Few by the Few for the Few

In spite of all the misgivings that followed the election of, and assumption of office by, Olusegun Obasanjo in 1999, there was relief that the Army was no longer in power and for politicians and civilians alike, the common enemy (the Army) - even though they could conceivably be more patriotic than some politicians - was gone and the scales were turned. The Army was no longer in power. The politicians and retired army officers, lying in wait for years, now controlled the local, state and federal governments as well as the councils, houses of Assembly and the National Assembly. It was inevitable that these leaders would fall apart like the old politicians when the negative bond of union was broken and removed. Personal rivalry and power struggle within the ranks of political parties and formations would again lead to imprisonment, victimization, death, retirement in the Army, private execution squads that would eliminate comrades-in-arms who jointly "liberated" the nation from the "tyranny of corrupt and arbitrary" Army Officers. Periodic parliamentary coups would un-sit or try to un-sit existing civilian State and National Assembly Speakers, Governors, and even the President instead of regular elections to effect a peaceful, democratic and constitutional change giving rise to a redefinition of Democracy in Nigeria as a government of the few, by the few for the sole benefit of the few.

Nigeria'S election 2003

In order to self-perpetuate oneself in office, the Constitution is manipulated, subverted and surreptitiously rewritten by the present regime. The Executive branch of Government bribes the Legislative arm to subvert the Constitution; the Legislative arm blackmails the executive into submission and collusion. The Judiciary stands defenseless and helpless in between. Local Government Elections in a studied collusion of disparate interests are postponed against the provisions of the Nation's Constitution. The people and the Government knew four years in advance that State and National elections were scheduled for 2003, yet no effort was made to revise the Electoral Register, order the ballot boxes and prepare for the inevitable.

When eventually voter registration started, many who registered could not find their names in the new revised Register now peopled with names from Harry Porter and Geoffrey Chaucer. The macabre dance of death continued and when elections came it was an inter-party and intra-party selection of the highest bidders as candidates hopped from one party to the other in search of undue advantages. The nomination in a majority of the parties was neither free nor fair. When elections did come, there was no voting in many places. Where votes were cast, they were never counted and where "stupidly" votes were counted, they were never recorded, and where they were recorded, they were never released and where they were released, losers were sometimes substituted as winners or depending on the position of the moon, people who were not nominated, who did not campaign, and who even were not on the ballot were brazenly declared and certified winners and Honourable members. **This rape of democracy must not be allowed to stand** for accepting this is tolling the death knell for Democracy not only in Nigeria but in the rest of black Africa. And now who is afraid of Local Government Elections in Nigeria?

On the Edge of a precipice

The present Civilian Governments of Nigeria on the Local, State and National levels have failed the people woefully. The hope that Nigeria's civilian leaders would accomplish for the nation what military rulers hungry for adulation at home and meteoric respect abroad failed to achieve has been dashed.... Nigeria, once again is being buffeted by the very same pressures and centrifugal forces that led to the demise of the regimes of Abubakar Tafawa Balewa, General Aguiyi Ironsi, General Gowon, General Murtala Muhamed, Alhaji Shehu Shagari, Generals Buhari and Idiagbon, General Babangida and General Sanni Abacha. Any Government that comes to power without the will and concurrence of the people is doomed to failure and for such a Government or collusion of State Governments to aspire unilaterally (outside a national conference) to rewrite the Nigerian constitution, abolish or review the Local Government System, drastically change the fundamental, directive principles of governance and abiding way of life of the Nigerian people, is a dismal exercise in futility doomed to quintessential failure.

We Should Learn From History

General Olusegun Obasanjo and the Peoples Democratic Party should learn from history, Nigeria's short history. What is done cannot be undone said Shakespeare once. The elections or selections have come and appear to have gone but not quite. General Obasanjo had the singular privilege of ruling Nigeria "against his own will" from 1975 to 1979, and again from 1999 to 2003 by the grace of God (a total of eight years of Nigeria's forty-three years of pseudo-independent existence). He would be tempting destiny and providence by now struggling to rule Nigeria against the will, and without the mandate, of the people from 2003 to 2007. There is for him a very narrow exit strategy, a window of opportunity that will forever immortalize his memory in the annals of Nigerian, African and black history.

A Narrow Exit Strategy

1. General Obasanjo should allow the Election Tribunals which his government appointed and controls to freely declare the recent electoral exercise null and void thus conferring a veneer of legality or necessity to the establishment of a provisional caretaker government..

2. General Obasanjo should stay in office provisionally until September 30, 2003, likewise the newly selected Governors on the State level.

3. General Obasanjo or any Governor who stays as caretaker ruler during the interim, should abstain from running for office as President or State Governor again; furthermore, should the President or any State Governor decide to run for Office again, he or she should hand over power immediately - to the Chief Justice of the Federation on the National Level and to the respective Chief Judge of the State on the state level.

4. Then the interim President, General Obasanjo or the Chief Justice of the Federation, should immediately sack the Chairman and Members of the Independent National Electoral Commission, convene beginning July 2003 a National Conference of all Political Parties and zonal stakeholders with a view to revising the Electoral Register and holding Local Govern-

ment, State and National Elections before December 2003. Any major Constitutional Review should be the work of the elected representatives of the people in a new National Assembly issuing from the December 2003 elections subject, of course, to the approval as provided for in the Constitution by the newly elected State Houses of Assembly.

This is a sacrifice, I know, that General Obasanjo can make for the nation and for future generations.

Four More Years of Obasanjo Will not Solve Nigeria's Problems

Truly, the problems of Nigeria cannot be solved in four years. This has been the erroneous miscalculation of a generation of military rulers, coup plotters and civilian politicians. In a dash of undue candour, an American analyst, on the eve of the Nigeria/Biafra war as General Odumegwu Ojukwu squared it off with General Gowon, had this to say: *"Now basically the Nigerian hasn't much sense. They cherish the fact they are running Nigeria, when, of course they are not. No country of this size and financial structure has much to say about its operation. The big money-men of the world who decide whether to invest or not; and the big governments of the world who decide whether or not to give aid, run just as much of Nigeria (or maybe more) than the Nigerians. You see, we quit colonizing by force but we colonize by money. If you will notice very carefully, all black countries are in this circumstance. They yelp wildly about their freedom and actually they have less freedom with domination by money than they had with colonial status."*

Consequent on this, smiling from the comfort of their distant chair and manipulation, foreign economic and political potentates help sow in Africa the seeds of discord where there is relative peace, and the flames of civil war where there is a misunderstanding. Naturally, this facilitates the cheap exploitation of Africa's natural resources: the oil of Nigeria, the uranium of the Congo, the diamond mines of Sierra Leone, the rubber in Liberia, the gold of Ghana and the vast riches of Angola. Thus Nigeria that sold her Bonny Light crude oil for thirty-five dollars a barrel in 1975 and flooded the country with **504** Peugeot Cars at five thousand Naira a unit was obligated, twenty-four years later, to give to its former colonial masters its oil, in January 1999, at ten dollars a barrel while paying four million Naira for a unit of almost the same **504** Peugeot Car. General Obasanjo, after four years in office, has probably realized that he could not solve the nation's problems in four years. Neither can he solve those problems in another four years. He will only compound them. After all, there must at least be one other Nigerian even in the Peoples Democratic Party who could run for the office of President instead of General Obasanjo.

Political Realism and Economic Exigency

No Nigerian, no matter how intelligent should have any illusions about solving the country's problems during his or her regime or even during one's life time. Nigeria's elastic needs like its population and problems expand with time. General Obasanjo, more than any Nigerian leader should bear witness to this fact. After all, General Obasanjo handed over to the civilian President of Nigeria Alhaji Shehu Shagari in 1979. Shehu Shagari ruled for four years and one Nigerian Naira was exchanging for US One Dollar fifty cents. General Buhari and General Idiagbon overthrew President Shagari again in 1983 accusing the government of ineptitude, corruption, and abysmal mismanagement of the economy. General Ibrahim Babangida overthrew his comrades-in-arms (Generals Buhari and Idiagbon) on August 27, 1985 accusing them of high-handedness, rudderless economic policies, draconian military decrees and inability to turn the economy and the nation around. Under Buhari and Idiagbon, one US Dollar exchanged for Six Nigerian Naira. General Babaginda ruled until he stepped aside unconquered, "unoverthrown" and unwanted in August 1993 and confessing his inability to comprehend why the Nigerian economy had not collapsed. Under him, the economy that was about picking up under Buhari/Idiagbon regime went from bad to worse and one US Dollar exchanged for Forty Naira.

General Sanni Abacha skillfully hop-stepped and jumped and succeeded General Babangida five months later after the Interim Government of the civilian Chief Ernest Shonekan in order to give a sense of direction to the nation and the economy. The thick-headed Nigerian economy went from being worse to downright chaotic (from bad to *mbadamba*) as one United States Dollar exchanged for one hundred and ten Naira. The end was not yet in sight. General Abacha and his team skillfully and energetically struggled and succeeded in pegging the Naira exchange rate at Eighty-three Naira to a Dollar at a time crude oil was selling at less than twelve dollars a barrel. Recently, under General Obasanjo, at a time crude oil, sold for between twenty-five dollars and thirty-two dollars a barrell, the Naira now exchanges for one hundred and forty Naira to a dollar with a negative growth in all the indices of the economy, and negative improvement in road infra-structure, with dwindling electricity generation, diminishing employment opportunities, problematic individual and collective security, troubling probity and accountability in government and parastatals, outright conversion of national assets into privatised domains; nationwide. The classrooms are empty with teachers and professors on strike, students helpless, graduates; there are decreasing educational opportunities, lower manpower utilization, increasing religious and social strife and for the few employed by the governments - unpaid salaries on the local, state and federal levels.

The World Bank and International Monetary Fund

Unfortunately for Nigeria and of course for Africa, the era of foreign aid has practically gone now replaced by foreign loans. Where before the US Agency for International Development under President John Fitzgerald Kennedy and under Secretary Williams provided the bulk of aid for the development of infrastructure and social services in Africa, the World Bank and International Monetary Fund stepped in with loans for projects battered by mismanagement and excessive corruption.

Economically the World Bank and the International Monetary Fund, to "salvage" these economies, imposed structural adjustment programs on Nigeria and Africa, declared all African currencies overvalued and insisted on the devaluation of the currencies of countries. These countries had little or nothing to export abroad and had to import basically all machinery and reprocessed raw materials for the manufacture of the few basic goods they produce. The World Bank and International Monetary Fund further insisted that the African economies throw their markets open at a time African rural farmers cannot compete with the mechanized farms and the overproductive capacity of Europe and America. Likewise, the cottage mini-industries of the black world could not compete with the automated production lines of the Western world.

Democracy like Austerity Should Have a Human Face

Nigeria today has one of the world's most vibrant economies and also one of the world's richest group of individuals but alas ranks as one of the world's lowest *per capita* income.

The problems of Nigeria today are therefore not merely economic. It stems from the inability of the leadership to manage Nigeria's economy for the good of the majority of people.

Legitimate and popular quest for democratization sowed the seeds of anarchy, endless strikes, social disruption and disintegration, and sometimes inordinate struggle by the elite for democratic power through undemocratic means. Meanwhile the common people in Nigeria and Africa face a slow death as some of their leaders grow fat with overseas personal and corporate accounts running into billions of dollars emanating from brazenly selective expropriation of the collective mineral wealth of the many by the few to the detriment of landowners and inhabitants. **Democracy** like **Austerity** should have a human face.

A New Wind of Change

This new inhuman face of government and democracy has exacerbated the inhumanity of men and women to one another. Today, Nigerian tribes have risen against tribes, clans against clans, and beliefs against beliefs, in pogroms no longer with matchets and arrows but with grenades and machine guns often sponsored by the so-called leaders and economic and political buccaneers. As it gradually now becomes apparent to all that the problem of Liberia was not alone the "villainy" of Samuel Doe or the "crude heroism" of Charles Taylor just as the problem of Nigeria was not solely the ineptitude of its leaders from Shehu Shagari through Buhari and Idiagbon, Babangida and Shonekan, Sanni Abacha and General Abubakar .... The problem of Chad was not Hissene Habre or Goukouni Weddeye, nor that of Burkina Faso the immaturity of Captain Thomas Sankara or his betrayal by his bosom friend and confidant Captain Blaise Campaore.

Poverty would continue to stare the common citizen in the face whether Nicephore Soglo or Colonel Mathieu Kerekou ruled Benin Republic and whether Konan Bedie or someone else replaced Houphouet Boigny in Cote d'Ivoire or Etienne Tshisikedi or Kabila took over from General Mobutu in Zaire. The villain, Idi Amin and the hero, Milton Obote have come and gone and Uganda is no closer to *Uhuru*. The absence of President Obiang Nguema Mbasogo may not improve the lot of the citizens of Equatorial Guinea nor would that of Albert Bernard Bongo guarantee democracy in Gabon.

Nigeria and Africa need new not necessarily young leaders, leaders that understand and share the philosophy of Dr. Kwame Nkrumah who speaking to his nation on January 23, 1966, on the occasion of the sad death of the former Prime Minister of Nigeria, Sir Abubakar Tafawa Balewa, said: "*The unhappy disputes which occurred from time to time between Nigeria and Ghana arose through Ghana's insistence on the immediate need for African unity as a necessary instrument for carrying forward Africa's struggle against imperialism, colonialism and neo-colonialism. The tragedy of Sir Abubakar was that he never realized that for Nigeria, the choice was either immediate political unification of Africa or Nigeria's disintegration. He scoffed at the idea of Africa unity. Thus he was destroyed by those very pressures and forces which only a continental government could have erased.*" Even today, the problems of Nigeria and other African States can only be solved within the context of a black African Government.

Time For New Leadership

The tide of economic and political progress in Africa has turned to the extent that today Africa pays more back to the World Bank and International Monetary Fund through debt servicing than it receives from those organizations for new programs even in repayable loans. Economic problems and the democratization process have brought several African countries to the verge of anarchy which is not a good substitute for inept leadership. Political vacuum should not be an alternative for a failed democracy. Some democratically elected governments in Africa have been just as repressive as the military dictatorships. A very thin and porous line separates for the common citizen the thirty years of Houphouet Boigny's civilian administration in Cote d'Ivoire and General Mobutu's thirty years of military government in Zaire. Democracy can only triumph and succeed where people are educated on the choices available, where people have access to the basic necessities of life. Talks of democracy and democratization are bound to fall on deaf ears in nations where eighty per cent of the people (mostly the young even when educated) are unemployed, unclothed, hungry, have no drinking water, poor housing, poorer schools, bad roads, no electricity, no fuel, no cooking gas or kerosine in the face of depleted woodlands, no drugs for the sick or money even to bury the dead and where eighty percent of the national wealth is spent on the emolument, fringe benefits and direct and indirect remuneration of a governing class comprising less than one percent of the population.

The needs of Nigeria today are basic and elemental.

The fact is that Nigeria like Africa is today impoverished. To survive, Nigeria and Africa must have to guard jealously its economic and political independence while remaining a part and parcel of the international community. Innocent peasants must not be punished because of the ineptitude and greed of their supposed leaders. The outside world if they are sincere in helping Africa must look beyond Africa's leaders and help promote those policies that will improve the education, health and the well-being of the common citizen.

Foreign governments should concentrate less on supporting those governments that facilitate their continued exploitation of developing economies because a serious crisis in Nigeria today will impact not just Africa as a whole but the entire world. Finally, General Obasanjo, the PDP State Governors and Peoples Democratic Party (PDP) should not be afraid of real and democratic local government elections. Power eventually belongs to the people and emanates from them. The power of truth when it erupts like a volcano, tends to engulf all who seek to mask it and unfortunately some of those who seek to unmask it.

CHAPTER 6

NIGERIA'S SE-LECTION IN 2007: CHRONICLE OF SHAME AND DECEIT

Nigerian Elections 2007 have come and gone. It was a chronicle of shame and deceit: shame to the country and deceit of the population. It must not be allowed to stand.

As early as December 2006, Nigerians knew and the world confirmed it that the Obasanjo's government and INEC (Independent National Electoral Commission) would not be ready for the election. Pierre-Richard Prosper, a former US Ambassador-at-Large for War Crime Issues, led a ten-man delegation from the International Republican Institute (IRI), Washington D. C that spend one week in Nigeria to assess the country's readiness for a free and fair election in April 2007. Prosper summed up their experiences in the following words: "We express grave concern over the fact that with only two weeks remaining before registration deadline, less than half of the machines needed to capture voter data electronically have arrived, let alone deployed to registration centers throughout the country. We are further concerned that only 3.5 million of the potential 60 million eligible voters have been registered as at the end of last week. ... The leadership of the INEC has set a noble and ambitious goal of implementing this cutting edge system to deter the past fraud in the registration efforts and the ensuing acrimony
 .... However, to meet the expectations of this goal on the time-table established is quite seriously in doubt, based on interviews with majority of those with whom we met. As a result, INEC is losing credibility with the general public . . . In its entire stay in Abuja, the delegation did not see one single poster with relevant information

mation, and our attempts to view a registration was stymied by the fact that no one knew how to locate one."

Yet the Government of Nigeria and Obasanjo claimed that it had invested the huge sum of N17 billion for the April 2007 general elections and N15 billion was claimed to have been given to the INEC chairman a week to the election. Dr. Maurice Iwu, INEC Chairman claimed to have awarded about 1000 contracts for the election supplies including the introduction of the Direct Data Capture Machine(DDC), that was "to prevent all loopholes that existed in the past for fraudulent politicians to rig elections." The DDC machines were neither available for registration purposes nor for the actual election.

An article, "Nigeria's Elections: Avoiding a Political Crisis," in *Africa Report* No. 123, Dakar/Brussels, on Wednesday, March 28, 2007, drew attention to the consequences of failure of the elections. "Failure could provoke violent rejection of the results by wide sections of the populace, denial of legitimacy and authority to the new government, intensification of the insurgency in the Niger Delta and its possible extension to other areas, with potential for wider West African destabilization. The preparatory phases have indicated failings in terms of basic fairness for the opposition, transparency and respect for the rule of law. Unless stakeholders make urgent efforts to rescue the credibility of the process, Nigeria's already serious internal instability could be fatally aggravated."

Warnings came from at home and abroad, including the Sultan of Sokoto, , Alhaji Mohammad Sa'ad Abubakar III, who on March 15, 2007 in Kaduna described the INEC as "unserious and ill-prepared for the April 2007 general elections," and warned about the dangers of a failed transition program. The Sultan added that in the face of INEC's "manifest un-seriousness," it was difficult to convince his subjects on the INEC's readiness "to conduct a free, fair and violence free elections." He concluded by emphasizing that "we will pray to the Almighty Allah to make it work because we need to have this election; we need to see through this transition so that we will not be a disgrace in the eyes of the world."

For the Presidential election, the INEC announced the following as candidates for the exercise:

Presidential Candidate	VP	Party
1. Prof. Patrick .O. Utomi -	Engr. Ibrahim Musa -	ADC
2. Sir Lawrence F. Adedoyin -	Alhaji Ali Abacha -	APS
3. Maj-Gen. M. Buhari (rtd) -	Hon. E. Ume-Ezeoke -	ANPP
4. Chief E. Osita Okereke -	Hajiya Asabe Mauna -	ALP
5. C. Odumegwu-Ojukwu	Alhaji Habib I. Gajo	APGA
6. Chief Adebayo Adefarati -	Alhaji Mahmud D. Sani	AD
7. Dr. Iheanyinchukwu Nnaji -	Dr. Adamu Musa -	BNPP
8. Maxi Okwu -	Hajiya R. Yasat Affah	CPP
9. Attahiru D. Bafarawa -	Engr. Ebere Udeogu -	DPP
10. Rev. Chris O. Okotie -	Fela Akinola Binutu -	FRESH
11. Chief Ambrose Owuru -	Alhaji Ibrahim Danjuma	HDP
12. M.Adekunle-Obasanjo	Mohammed Abdullahi	MMN
13. Dr. Oladapo Agoro -	Eghenayheore Dele Ayi	NAC
14. Dr. Osagie O. Obayuwana -	Mal. Yunusa S. Tanko	NCP
15. Alhaji Aliyu Habu-Fari	Chudi C. Chukwuani	NDP
16. Dr. Akpone Solomon-	Alj Abdullahi Abdullahi	NMDP
17. Mal. Aminu G. Abubakar -	Kingsley Onye-Eze Ibe	NUP

18. Prof. Isa Odidi   O. Akeem-Bello   ND
19. Galtima Baboyi Liman -   Abitti Onoyom Ndok   NNPP
20. Dr. Brimmy A. Olaghere -   Mal. Zainab G. Bayero   NPC
21. Umaru Musa Yar'Adua -   Dr. Goodluck Jonathan   PDP
22. Arthur Nwankwo -   Mohammed Abdullahi   PMP
23. Orji Uzor Kalu -   Inuwa Abdulkadir   PPA
24. Chief Sunny J. Okogwu   Hajia Larai Umaru   RPN

Of course, the elections in the component states and Abuja came on April 14, 2007 for the Gubernatorial and State Assembly posts and on April 21 for the Senate, House of Representatives and Presidential posts. The rigging surpassed worst fears of many. I was not there present physically. Hence I have complied these reports from Nigerians and foreigners who were eye witnesses of this crime against humans and humanity. See S. Okechukwu Mezu. *Nigerian Elections 2007: Chronicle of Shame and Deceit.* Baltimore: Black Acacdemy Press, Inc. 2007.

The 2007 Movement of the Nigeria House of Representatives has this to say about the elections: "By any standard, this election cannot be called free, or fair, much less credible. It was a predetermined systema-tically orchestrated exercise that was out to return the ruling party at all cost. The barbarism, violation, etc, were as outrageous as they were unprecedented. We therefore reject the result in its entirety and call for another fresh election under a reconstituted INEC, and after the 29th of May 2007, when President Olusegun Obasanjo must have left....This undoubtedly is the worst election in the history of this country. This is the greatest disservice to democracy as it is capable of not only undermining it, but also in fact derailing and crippling our democracy altogether."

Foreign election observers and observers from Nigeria have confirmed that this is probably the worst election ever not only in Nigeria but in the history of electoral democracy. The electoral crimes ranged from the stuffing of ballot boxes, to the hijacking, of ballot papers. Several polling stations were not opened. The ones that opened had no ballot boxes. During the gubernatorial and state assembly elections, many people lost their lives; there was thuggery and burning; intimidation using state security services was unleashed to stymie opposition.

During the Presidential elections, it has been adduced that more than seventy percent of the sixty million ballot papers (printed in South Africa at the very last minute by INEC for the Presidential election) were deliberately abandoned in the cargo wing of the airport in Johannesburg, South Africa. This means that about eighteen million ballot papers only were delivered in Nigeria for the sixty million prospective registered voters. Since these arrived in Nigeria on the very night before the election, how were these delivered to the nooks and corners of Nigeria's 923,768 square kilometers stretching from the Gulf of Guinea and Atlantic Ocean (Bights of Benin and Biafra) to areas bordering with Cameroon in the East and Chad in the North-East, Niger in the North, and Benin Republic to the West. How were these ballot papers and election materials delivered over night to the low coastal zone, the hills and plateaus of the Center, to the mountainous zones of the East, some between 1,200 and 2,042 meters high and this including the riverine areas of the Delta region and the impassable gullies of the hinterland.

I was not there, so I will leave Nigerian and foreign journalists and reporters to tell the story in their own words. We dedicate this work to them for some lost their lives and others paid with their property. The Nigerian elite have been called upon to lead the resistance against this evil election that desecrated all that is noble and glorious about government of the people by the people. Silence is complicity. This farce of an election and an open rape of democracy must not be allowed to stand. Nigerians were urged by the world to tolerate and accept the sham election of 1999 that installed Olusegun Obasanjo as President against the votes of the people and against their wishes. They were rewarded with the inglorious catastrophe that was the 2003 Nigerian **S-election** which gave rise to my lead article in that book "Who is Afraid of Local Government Elections," published in several media in 2003. Corruption and greed on the part of some and powerlessness on the part of others, interminable litigation in election tribunals for over thirty months, assassinations and suppresion, oppression victimization, dehumanization and incarceration of opponents, emasculated a courageous opposition, some of whom paid with their lives, while others paid with their property.

We argued then that the 2007 election must not be allowed to stand for letting that election to stand would be enthroning barbarism and hooliganism that will destroy and disintegrate not only Nigeria but could spill all over Africa during any future attempt at a so-called "democratic" election in the country. And of course, it will then affect the West, the East, the North, the South and the World. Prevention is better than cure. This criminality must not be allowed to stand and every intellectual must use whatever weapon at his or her disposal to fight it.

Finally, in *"Postscript: Which Way, Nigeria,"* the last chapter in the book, *Nigerian Elections 2007: Chronicle of Shame and Deceit,* I tried to present concrete proposals as a way out of the predicament then: an interim government headed by the Chief Judge of the Federation on a national level and Chief Judge of the State on the local level; a new INEC, encouraging the emergence of three to four political parties with the possibility of independent candidates under prescribed conditions, registration of voters and digitalization of its display, printing of ballots in Nigeria, election of a Constituent Assembly before March 2008

CHAPTER 7

VICE PRESIDENT GOODLUCK JONATHAN OF NIGERIA:
National Assembly Resolution and the Transfer of Power

WHAT THE NIGERIAN CONSTITUTION SAYS:

Supposedly, it was the constitution of the Federal Republic of Nigeria that created the National Assembly (Senate and House of Representatives), the Executive Branch (President, Vice President and Federal Executive Council of the Federal Republic of Nigeria) and the electoral laws and the organ Independent National Election Commission (INEC) that conducted the elections that brought the present occupants to power. There were of course no elections in 2007 but a chronicle of shame and deceit .. . This is not the subject of this article. The crucial question here is - does that National Assembly have the legal standing to transfer the way it did to the Vice President of Nigeria the powers of the President of the Federation? The answer is a decided **NO**. It is illegal, *ultra vires*, null, void and of no effect.

The motion which was presented by Senator Folarin and seconded by Senator Ike Ekweremadu read thus:

"The Senate notes that the President, Commander-in-Chief of the Armed Forces of the Federation, His Excellency, Alhaji Umaru Yar'Adua, GCFR, left Nigeria for a medical attention in the Kingdom of Saudi Arabia on the 23rd November 2009.

"Notes that the entire country, particularly the Senate, prayed for his quick recovery and expected his early return from the said medical vacation.

"Notes that on the 12th of January 2010, His Excellency, President Umaru Yar'Adua, GCFR, transmitted to the whole world through the British Broadcasting Corporation (BBC), a declaration that he is receiving medical treatment in Saudi Arabia and consequently will be unable to discharge the func-

tions of his office until his doctors certify him fit to return to Nigeria to assume his duties.

"Notes that the President of the Senate and the Speaker of the House of Representatives read the President's declaration transmitted through the BBC and further published in several print media.

"Satisfied that, in the interest of our nation, Section 145 of the Constitution of the Federal Republic of Nigeria 1999 has been complied with by the said declaration.

"Do hereby resolve as follows:

1. That the Vice-President, His Excellency Dr. Goodluck Ebele Jonathan, GCON, shall henceforth discharge the functions of the office of the President, Commander-in-Chief of the Armed Forces of the federation as Acting President.

2. That the Vice-President shall cease to discharge the functions of the office of the President when the President pursuant to Section 145 of the Constitution of the Federal Republic of Nigeria 1999 transmits to the President of the Senate and the Speaker of the House of Representatives in writing that he has returned from his medical vacation."

DISHONESTY BREEDS DISHONESTY

It is flabbergasting to read that when the Senate President put the question, it was "unanimously agreed to." Are there no men or women of integrity in the Senate of the National Assembly? Rather than stabilize the polity, it has commenced another dance of death and destruction for Nigeria. What the Constitution states is clear, unequivocal, unambiguous and specific. Section 144 (1) of Nigeria's constitution states:

The President or Vice-President shall cease to hold office, if—

(a) by a resolution passed by two-third majority of all members of the executive council of the Federation it is declared that the President or Vice-President is incapable of performing the functions of his office; and

(b) the declaration is verified, after such medical examination as may be necessary, by a medical panel established under subsection (4) of this section in its report to the President of Senate and the Speaker of the House of Representatives.

Subsection (4) states that: The medical panel to which this section relates shall be appointed by the President of the Senate, and shall comprise five medical practitioners in Nigeria—
  (a) one of whom shall be a personal physician of the holder of the office concerned; and

(b) four other medical practitioners who have in the opinion of the President of the Senate, attained a high degree of eminence in the field of medicine relative to the nature of the examination to be conducted in accordance with the foregoing provisions.

Subsection (2) provides as follows: Where the medical panel certifies in the report that in its opinion the President or Vice-President is suffering from such infirmity of body or mind as renders him permanently incapable of discharging the functions of his office, a notice thereof signed by the President of the Senate and Speaker of the House of Representatives shall be published in the Official Gazette of the Government of the Federation.

Subsection (3) states:

The President or Vice-President shall cease to hold office as from the date of publication of the notice of the medical report pursuant to subsection (2) of this section."

VICE PRESIDENT GOODLUCK JONATHAN

A two-third majority of all members of the executive council of the Federation has not declared that the President is incapable of performing the functions of his office; the declaration was not verified and no medical panel was set up as under sub-section (3); neither was there a notice signed by the President of the Senate and Speaker of the House of Representatives published in the Official Gazette of the Government of the Federation to that effect. What happened was not the creation of a legal precedent or legal antecedent but adventurism towards the edge of a great precipice. It is the executive council of the Federation made up of the Vice President and Ministers, as described in section 144 (5) that should initiate the process. But a government that comes into power through the subversion of the democratic electoral process will produce nothing but subversion of the constitution and the democratic process. Loyalty to self interest takes precedence over loyalty to the nation. Just as Ministers produced through and from a flawed process cannot be expected to stand by the truth so also Honorable members produced from a dishonorable undemocratic process cannot be expected to stand by the truth, live by the truth and vote on the basis of what is right not what is expedient.

DAYS OF INFAMY

It was most shocking and disappointing that not even a single member of the Executive Council of the Federation dissented when Judge Abutu ventured to force them to vote within two weeks in accordance with section 144 (1) (a) in the absence of a proper adherence to section 145 of the constitution and laws of the Federation. It is incongruous that the Senate of the Federation based its decision on the purported Yar'Adua interview supposedly with the BBC some four weeks earlier saying that he would resume duty when his doctors so certify. If they are to be believed, why did it take them four weeks to absorb the "import" of this unverified message to a foreign British organ, not even to the Vice President, President of the Senate, Speaker of the House of Representatives or even the Nigerian press. Members of the Federal Executive Council, without seeing the President, without speaking to him, without consulting with the President's doctors "unanimously" voted and confirmed that the President was not incapacitated. Not even one voice dissented. The Dora Akunyili, *post ipso facto* rethink is a *mea culpa* and not a profile in courage. We certainly thank God that she reclaimed her integrity. She was a unique and a saving grace. In a reverse mode, the House of Representatives after maintaining a few days earlier that President Musa Yar'Adua was hale and hearty enough to continue in office joined their Senate Confreres-in-Ignominy to affirm that power should be transmitted to Vice President Goodluck Jonathan to act as President and Commander-in-Chief of the Armed Forces of the Federal Republic of Nigeria. Were these Honorable members oblivious of the BBC broadcast a few weeks earlier? Honor and integrity should be made of sterner stuff. The Executive Council of the Federation has failed the nation. Their crime, while unpardonable, is understandable because they are appointed by President Yar'Adua. The National Assembly has failed the nation. Their lapses, while inconceivable, are explainable because they were not elected by the people. At least one Judge, Justice Abutu of the Federal High Court, Abuja, in the Judiciary has failed the nation by doing the bidding of the the Attorney-General, Michael Aondoakaa who believes that the President can rule Nigeria from anywhere in the world even from a Hospital Intensive

Care Unit (ICU) in Saudi Arabia. Justice Dan Abutu purported to direct the Vice-President to expressly take over power in the absence of the President pending his recovery and return to office contrary to the provisions of Section 145 of the 1999 constitution which only permits the Vice President to discharge the functions of President as Acting President only and only if the President transmits a letter in accordance with section 145 or in the alternative assume the functions of an Acting President as envisioned in section 145 or the functions of the President according to section 146 if and only if the President is absent by reason of death or resignation, impeachment, permanent incapacitation (in accordance to section 144) or finally by the President's removal from office for any other reason in accordance to sections 143 and 144.

AONDOAKAA SOPHISTRY:
American and Nigerian Presidential Systems

Aondoakaa in his skewed syllogism compares the Nigerian Presidential system to the American system. He observed in a session with State House Correspondents that Nigeria practices a presidential system of government very identical to that of the US. He spoke about the provisions of the 25th Amendment to the US Constitution which is similar to the provisions of Section 145 of the 1999 Constitution of Nigeria. *"Since the history of America, that provision has been used three times. The first person to assume office under the provision of the voluntary transfer of power was President G. Bush Senior. He became the first person in the history of America to be an acting president."* He mentioned the case on July 13, 1985 when President Ronald Regan went for colon cancer surgery, transmitted a letter to the Speaker of the House of Representatives and the President of the Senate intimating them of his incapacity leading to the Vice President George Bush acting as President from 11:28 a.m. to 7:22 p.m. of the same day. Following the end of the operation, Ronald Regan transmitted another letter and assumes power as President. Attorney General Aoandoakaa mentioned the case on June 29, 2002 when President George Bush Jr declared himself temporarily unable to discharge the power of the president and the duties of his office because he was undergoing surgery, which required sedation. President Bush Jr. followed the established protocol and Vice President Dick Cheney acted from 7:09 a.m. to 9:24 a.m. A similar routine was also followed from 7:16 a.m. to 9:21 a.m. on July 22, 2007 when President George Bush underwent another surgery which required sedation.

Attorney General Aondoakaa having given these laudable examples, in the worst sophistry known to the human mind, pretends not to see the necessity for a President (in an Intensive Care Unity (ICU) even if periodically since November 23, 2009, for a period of more than seventy days in far away Saudi Arabia) to do what is right, honorable and expedient, that is, to follow the law, before his departure, or during his stay in Saudi Arabia by writing to the National Assembly for the peaceful and quiet transfer of power to his Vice President for the smooth running of Government as enshrined in the Constitution of the Federal Republic of Nigeria. And if the President is unable or unwilling, the Attorney General Aondoakaa failed and/or neglected to advise the Executive Council of the Federation properly to do the right thing; and no member of the Executive Council until the revolt led by Lady Dora Akunyili saw it right and proper to show fidelity to the nation and its Constitution. We must here excuse the Vice President Goodluck Jonathan who cannot be an advocate and beneficiary of the advocacy at the same time.

JUDICIARY, LEGISLATURE AND SEPARATION OF POWER

So, when on January 22, 2010 Justice Dan Abutu, Chief Judge of the Federal High Court, ruled on suit No

FHC/ABJ/654/2010 and directed the Executive Council of the Federation, to within 14 days, consider, pass and publicize a resolution in accordance with the provisions of Section 144 of the 1999 constitution declaring whether, having regard to the absence of the President from Nigeria on medical ground since the 23rd of November 2009, the President is incapable of discharging the functions of his office," appeared to give legal backing to a cause pre-scripted by the Attorney General of the Federation. Aondoakaa was emboldened in his syllogism: *"We cannot and no organ of government can take over the responsibilities of the court, which is supposed to be the law. If the court gives a decision, it is not open to anybody or organ of government to say that the court is wrong. The only position left is that if you are affected by the decision of the court, if you are not a party to the case; you apply for leave as an interested party to appeal against the decision of the court as an interested party. That decision gives the VP unencumbered power to act on his behalf and at least that is what we have so far and that should be the guiding consideration of all of us which could have been if we are obeying rule of law and not subjecting the decision of the court to undue political consideration, that could have ended the matter. On the part of the executive council we have accepted the decision of the court and as long as we know, no minister can disagree with the VP and no executive order issued by the VP can be questioned by any authority in the executive arm of government. That is the position."*

The court is not the law. The Law in this case is the Constitution of the Federal Republic of Nigeria. The court only interprets the law; it does not and should not make law. That is the duty of the National Assembly. The court cannot and should not confer on the Vice President and give him "unencumbered power to act" on the behalf of the President. The Federal Executive Council should therefore not accept the decision of the court as advocated by Aondoakaa.

In the United States which Aondoakaa sees as akin to the Nigerian system, under Section 3 of the 25th Amendment, the president may transfer the presidential powers and duties to the vice president, who then becomes acting president by transmitting a statement to the Speaker of the House and the president *pro tempore* of the Senate stating the reasons for the transfer. The president resumes the discharge of the presidential powers and duties when he transmits, to those two officials, a written declaration stating that resumption. This transfer of power occurred for reasons President Bush considered appropriate in 2002 and again in 2007 as rightly pointed out by Attorney General Aondoakaa for medical procedures that required sedation following which President Bush resumed power the same day. President Musa Yar'Adua failed and/or neglected to follow this protocol available in the Nigerian constitution.

US 25TH AMENDMENT
AND SECTION 144 OF NIGERIA'S CONSTITUION

Also, under Section 4 of the 25th Amendment to the US Constitution, the vice president and a majority of the Cabinet (in Nigeria, Executive Council of the Federation) may transfer the presidential powers and duties from the president to the vice president once they transmit to the Speaker of the House and the president *pro tempore* of the Senate a statement declaring the president's incapacity to discharge the presidential powers and duties. When this happens, the vice president assumes the presidential powers and duties as acting president but the president can declare that no such inability exists and resume the discharge of the presidential powers and duties. Where the vice president and the cabinet contest this claim, then the US Congress must meet within two days whether in session or not to examine and decide the merit of the conflicting claims. Here again the Executive Council of the Federation failed the Nigerian nation by culpably refusing to uphold the constitution they swore to defend. The National Assembly also failed Nigerians by refusing to carry out the duties assigned to them by the Constitution. Both members of the Federal Executive Council and the National Assembly who aided and abetted this rape of the constitution should be tried for treason and if found guilty the two institutions should stand dissolved and individuals found to have conspired to aid and abet this rape of democracy should be banned from holding political office, if not for life, at least for a period of five years.

It is not too late to do the right and intelligent thing. The act of both Houses of the National Assembly passing separate motions authorizing the handing-over of power to the Vice-President Goodluck Jonathan and asking him to take over as "Acting President and the Commander-in-chief of the Nigeria Armed Forces" until such a time that Umaru Yar'Adua returns from medical treatment in Saudi Arabia and transmits a letter indicating that he is medically fit to resume his duties, has no place in law or the constitution of Nigeria. And who swears in Acting President Goodluck Jonathan? Is it the Chief Justice of the Federation who was sworn in before his time? No one should hold responsible for the impasse the sick and incapacitated President Musa Yar'Adua. Former President Olusegun Obasanjo was not quite fair to President Yar'Adua when he opined in one of his frank outbursts: *"If you take up an appointment, a job, elected, appointed, whatever it is, and then your health starts failing and you will not be able to deliver to satisfy yourself and satisfy the people who you are supposed to serve, then there is a path of honour you are supposed to take .... There is a path of honour and morality and if you don't know that then you don't know anything."* A human being in an intensive care unit cannot be held responsible for his actions or inactions. Neither is a human being under serious sedation aware of, or concerned with, issues of "honor" and "morality."

MORALITY, HONOR AND JURISPRUDENCE

Demola Seriki, Minister of State, Interior, on the other hand was equally wrong when he postulates: *"The Constitution of the Federal Republic of Nigeria which we operate is very clear on certain things. First, when people ask the National Assembly to act, they miss the point. The National Assembly can only act in line with this Constitution of Nigeria .... Then people say those in the Federal Executive Council, FEC, are not mindful of the feelings of Nigeria, that Section 144 of the Constitution of the Federal Republic of Nigeria has taken care of it. I ask those saying so, have they read it? If they have read it, do they understand it? That section, that is Section 144, convenient as it is for those quoting it, says the FEC should act in a situation of permanent incapacitation. My question is: Are we there yet? .... When people quote the Constitution, they should quote it well and not the way it suits their desires."*

Nigerians have not only read the Constitution of the Federal Republic of Nigeria, they understand it very well. Insanity no matter how temporary is still insanity. Incapacity, permanent or not, no matter its duration is incapacity within that limited time, space and spectrum. Sedation, even for a duration of a few hours (as in the case of President George Bush in the US) tolls Section 144 of the Nigerian Constitution. Absence of President Yar'Adua from November 23, 2009 and counting – incommunicado, unseen, unheard – cries to the highest heavens for action.

Those around President Yar'Adua who seek to use his name to cling to power should be held accountable. It is believed that only his wife and maybe two close aides have access to him. We wish him God's blessing and speedy recovery. But he is not just a husband and father, he is a public figure, the father of the nation. His health is the health of the nation; his sickness portends a sick nation. The people and the nation have as much right as the immediate family to know the truth and nothing but the truth about the state of his health. Nature abhors vacuum and there should be none in the Presidency but the right thing should be done.

STATE OF THE NATION AND THE WAY FORWARD

The purported letter from the National Assembly dated February 10, 2010, and addressed to the Chief Justice of Nigeria, Justice Ignatius Katsina-Alu, the Executive Council of the Federation (EXCOF) and the Acting President referenced as NASS/C5/R/05/III/92 from the Clerk of the National Assembly, Mr. Yemi Ogunyomi, to the Secretary to the Government of the Federation far from solving the debacle confounds it. Titled as **'State Of The Nation And The Way Forward - National Assembly Resolutions, Of 9th, February, 2010'**, it says:

"*On Tuesday 9 February, 2010, the Senate and House of Representatives adopted Resolutions on the State of the Nation occasioned by the prolonged medical holidays of the President, Commander-in-Chief of the Armed Forces, His Excellency, Alhaji Umaru Yar'Adua in the Kingdom of Saudi Arabia.*

"*Members of the National Assembly noted that Nigerians fervently prayed for the speedy recovery of Mr. President and his early return to Nigeria.*

"*However, on 12 January 2010, Mr. President informed Nigerians through the British Broadcasting Corporation (BBC), that he was receiving medical treatment in Saudi Arabia, and would only return to Nigeria to resume his functions as President when his doctors so certify.*

"*Satisfied that this declaration by Mr. President amounts to substantial compliance with the provision of Section 145 of the Constitution of Nigeria 1999, the National Assembly resolved that:*

(i) the Vice President, His Excellency Dr. Goodluck Ebele Jonathan, shall henceforth discharge the functions of the Office

of the President, Commander-in-Chief of the Armed Forces of the Federation as Acting President; and

(ii) the Vice President shall cease to discharge the functions of the Office of the President when the President, Commander-in Chief of the Armed Forces of the Federation, transmits to the President of the Senate and the Speaker of the House of Representatives in writing, that he has returned from his medical vacation.

"Kindly convey these National Assembly Resolutions to His Excellency, Dr. Goodluck Ebele Jonathan, the Chief Justice of the Federation for his information, and Members of the Federal Executive Council for compliance.

"Find attached hereto, the Votes and Proceedings of the Senate and the House of Representatives in this regard, please.

"Accept the assurances of my highest regards for your office."

The Resolution is null and void and of no effect with due regard to the provisions of the Nigerian Constitution and even if it is passed off as law of the National Assembly, who signs it to give it the due effect as prescribed by the Constitution - the incapacitated President or the Acting beneficiary of the incapacitation. The separation of powers does not allow the National Assembly or its Secretary to give directives to the Judiciary, or to the Executive arm of government, certainly not to the members of the Federal Executive Council just as the Secretary to the Government of the Federation cannot give directives for compliance to the staff of the National Assembly. "Acting" President Goodluck Ebere Jonathan should realize that the Jerusalem crowd that sang **Hossana, Hossana** on Sunday was the same crowd a short Friday later that shouted **Crucifixi eum, crucifixi eum. Crucify Him! Crucify Him!**

Monday, 15 February 2010 00, by Dr. S. Okechukwu Mezu

CHAPTER 8

**Dr. S. Okechukwu Mezu's Message
to Nigerians in the Diaspora
Our Contract with Imo State Citizens
<u>MANIFESTO: Short Term and Long Term Goals</u>**

*(Being the text of a speech delivered by **Dr. S. Okechukwu Mezu, Deputy Gubernatorial Candidate (Imo State) of Congress for Progressive Change (CPC)** during the Rally/Dinner of Imo Citizens in the Diaspora in Baltimore, Maryland on Friday February 18, 2011 at the America Best Inn, 6510 Frankford Avenue, Baltimore, Maryland 21206, USA.). Chukwuemeka Nwajiuba was the Gubernatorial Candidate of the CPC in Imo State.*

It is my great pleasure to welcome you to this event to night. Approximately forty three years ago (in 1967), great challenges confronted the Igbos of Nigeria with the *coup d'etat* of January 15, 1966 led by Chukwuma Kaduna Nzeogwu an outstanding progressive, who was buried with full military honors when killed by those he fought against. His *coup d'etat* was triggered by political lawlessness, uncontrolled looting of the treasury in the political arena and uncontrolled looting and lacing in the streets of Western Nigeria. Unfortunately the Sarduana of Sokoto, Sir Ahmadu Bello, the Prime Minister of Nigeria, Sir Tafawa Balewa and the Finance Minister, Chief Festus Okotie Eboh (among others including military officers) were killed in the process. The pogrom of Igbos followed in Northern Nigeria beginning in July 1966 - atrocities we would rather not recount but will never forget.

I was then completing my Doctoral dissertation at The Johns Hopkins University, here in Maryland. As a young man, I led demonstrations in front of the US State Department in Washington D.C. to protest the murder in the Congo of Prime Minister Patrice Lumumba. I believed in Pan-African Unity (in fact organized an International Conference on Pan-Africanism as President of the Organization of African and American Students. The proceedings of that conference was edited by me and published in 1964 by Georgetown University Press.) Beyond Pan-African Unity, we believed in a Pan Black world inspired by William DuBois, Marcus Garvey, Booker T. Washington, Kwame Nkrumah, Nnamdi Azikiwe, Julius Nyerere, and those I celebrated in my book *Black Leaders of the Centuries* published in 1970.

The war broke out in 1967. Biafra and the Igbos were attacked and faced liquidation through starvation and blockade from the sea, the air and the land. Many of us were conflicted. Can a committed Pan-Africanist like me really support the secession of Biafra from Nigeria. For me the choice was clear and immediate. I was offered an appointment as a Senior Diplomat by Chief Simeon Adebo, Nigeria's Representative at the United Nations. After a night in his house and as his guest at the Ambassador's Residence in the elegant suburb of New York, my mind was made up. I must fight for the defense of my people.

I postponed the defense of my Doctoral dissertation which I had written in Paris as an exchange student at the *Ecole Pra-*

tique des Hautes Etudes, a joint program of the University of Paris with The Johns Hopkins University. Together with Ambassador Ralph Uwechue, we founded the Biafra Historical Research Society in Paris (a pseudonym for the Biafran Embassy in Europe, from where we organized the steady supply of food and medicine through *Caritas Internationalis*, International Red Cross, *Terre des Hommes* for the beleaguered citizens of Biafra. I hereby confess that we also sent planes, arms and ammunition through other sources for the defense of Biafra and its citizens. I was later appointed by General Ojukwu following the recognition of Biafra by Cote d'Ivoire as the Biafran Ambassador to Ivory Coast and President Houphouet-Boigny with concurrent accreditation to Anglophone West Africa and to President Leopold Sedar Senghor of Senegal whose works and life (incidentally) was the subject of my Doctoral dissertation. *Leopold Sedar Senghor et la defense et illustration de la civilization noire* (Paris 1968).

I had the honor and privilege of being a member of the Biafran Delegation to Niamey (Niger Republic) Peace Conference under President Hamani Diori (1968) and the OAU sponsored Addis Ababa (Ethiopia) Conference (1968) under the Chairmanship of Emperor Haile Selassie. This was the final effort by General Ojukwu and General Gowon to settle the conflict at the Conference Table. The night before the Conference, I translated into French and had printed General Ojukwu's speech for simultaneous distribution in French and English following its delivery. The rest is history and even though General Gowon, a good man, promised *"No Victor, No Vanquished,"* the Igbos were not only defeated but were vanquished and treated as such but their heads were unbowed.

On January 15, 1973, my wife (Dr. Rose Ure Mezu) and I and our three children (Chinyere, Nnenna and Obinna) left Buffalo, New York where I was Professor of French and Founder/Director of the African Studies Program at the State University of New York and landed in Nigeria where I was offered appointment as Professor of French and Chairman, Modern Languages Department, a Member of the Senate of the University of Nigeria, Nsukka (the youngest ever in the history of that University). My wife, Dr. Rose Mezu, was also appointed Lecturer at the University. We instead went home to my village, Ezeogba in Emekuku, Owerri, my town (without running water or electricity) except from the generator I shipped in from the United States which then provided the only point of light between Owerri and Umuahia (a distance of forty miles). Owerri was then serviced by Electricity Corporation of Nigeria (ECN).

Rather than accept employment and the comfort of a University setting, even then dilapidated after the war, I chose to go back to my people to create employment and was able following some years of hard and determined work to create employment for over two hundred and fifty people by setting up a Printing and Publishing Company, a Cosmetics Manufacturing Company, a Building and Major Road Construction Company, Plastic Industries (Emekuku and Aba), Foundation Insurance Company (Life and Non-Life), Emekuku Community Bank (one of the first ten in Nigeria to be commissioned), a Real Estate Company, Guest Houses, Supermarket, Saloons and Holiday Resorts. By 1996, I closed down all these facilities and relocated to the United States with my family to make sure my children did not become less educated than their parents for at one point the Universities in Nigeria were closed indefinitely. That mission, I believe, has been accomplished and now the Fatherland calls again not for what it can do for me but for what I strongly believe I can do for the people.

People in government in Nigeria today on the Local Government level, State Government level and Federal level have lost focus. *"Onye anughi oge eliri mmadu, ji esi ukwu na avo ya"* an Igbo saying insists. *When a grave has no marker, any-*

one not present during the burial is unable to distinguish the location of the head or the feet. We (in Imo State) are worse off today (2011) than we were thirty years ago (1981). Then there was pipe borne water every where (Owerri, Orlu, Okigwe). We had Amaraku Power generation plant supplying electricity to the state. We had the Aluminum Extrusion plant at Inyishi, Paint Industry in Mbaise, Shoe Industry at Owerri, Clay and Burnt brick industry at Ezinachi, Golden Guinea Breweries, Ceramics Industry, Glass Industry in the then Greater Imo State. We had a functional education system, a functioning Imo State University, a clean urban environment, functioning hospitals, Imo Newspapers Limited. As Chairman of Imo Newspapers Limited, I raised within six months the circulation from 50,000 to 150,000. Today that newspaper is a relic of the past and unseen at newspaper kioks.

These strides made thirty years ago are gone replaced by sub-standard mini generating sets, agents of deadly pollution; replaced by dry water pipes that have not seen water for years; and of course by family untested boreholes in every well-off home. Children of the well-to-do are now sent to expensive private elementary and high schools or abroad for those who can afford it. The brain drain has assumed alarming proportions. You are all here evidence of this drain. Those in the diaspora who dare to go back to Imo State and come home to help (even on Medical missions) are either kidnapped or unappreciated. Imo State sons overseas are afraid to go home and bury their parents; dutiful daughters uproot their aged mothers and bring them in desperation to America for basic medical and health needs that could have been taken care of at a General Medical Practitioner's office.

Who will bell the cat? If we, my dying and receding generation cannot do so, then all hope is lost for the millions of Igbo and Nigerian children, grandchildren and great grandchildren we have here in America and abroad. The fate of the parents, siblings and relations they have at home becomes more problematic. The situation is even then worse for those at home – university graduates from four years ago who have no job, and worse still no hope; those who have jobs and are never paid and when paid, never on time; the pensioners who suffer degradation to collect their monthly allocation years in arrears stretchered on the back of their son or a relation - and some die on the footsteps of the Government Treasury unable to lift their hands to collect their miserly pay for over thirty years of service to the state. Civil servants tend to forget that the youthful civil servant of today is the maltreated pensioner of tomorrow. Let us make life better for one another and not create hell, in the words of Albert Camus, for one another: *Nous sommes l'enfer les uns pour les autres.*

Nigerians cannot for ever live in the Ivory Tower that is America, London, Paris and Abuja and forget the deplorable and miserable conditions of our people at home, the sick, the homeless, the aged – even the forlorn look of desperation of the unemployed able-bodied. We must make the sacrifice to change the situation at home, in Imo State, in Nigeria, in Africa and the black world. We must all be engaged. And if the sacrifice we make is not painful, then it is not enough. If for family and personal reasons, we cannot take part in the elections as candidates, let us do all we can to support those candidates that will bring to fruition our ideals, our aspirations, our objectives. Hon. Chukwuemeka Nwajiuba and I, Dr. S. Okechukwu Mezu, are in this to win not for ourselves but for the people, for the nation.

Let me just briefly address the issue of education and health since our detailed manifesto has been posted on our website: www.cpcimostate.org.

Education

Illiteracy is the bane of progress because good education is a sure ticket to enlightenment, employment and a good quality of life. Our strategy for the educational sector is to:

- Establish partnerships between our local universities and world class educational institutions in different parts of the world to facilitate information exchange, capacity building, knowledge sharing, and research partnerships in all fields including health, public health, engineering, computing, management sciences to mention a few.
- Establish **four year colleges** in each Senatorial zone of Imo State (Okigwe, Orlu and Owerri) to serve as feeder institutions to the Imo State University Center and Professional Colleges at the State Capital.
- Establish **two-year colleges** in each Local Government Area of Imo State to serve as feeder institutions to the four-year colleges at the Senatorial Centers. These institutions will naturally create additional direct and indirect employment for our citizens.
- Rehabilitate the primary and secondary education system by setting up continuing education credit systems through which teachers are armed with up-to-date strategies and knowledge for teaching.

Health Care
- Improvement of the Health care system by implementation of an Emergency Response system.
- Improving and reforming our State Hospitals and providing ensuring quality care to all citizens. We should not just take pride in the establishment of a Teaching Hospital at Orlu, Imo State, a first class hospital the equivalent of a Teaching Hospital will be established in each Senatorial zone and a Comprehensive Community Hospital in each Local Government Area.
- We shall make these zonal hospitals centers of excellence with the provision of State-of-the-art diagnostic and medical equipment like Xray machines, Ultrasound, Ct-scans, MRI's and modern operating rooms.
- Such zonal hospitals shall have functional specialized medical units with Neonatal Intensive Care Units (NICU), Med-

ical Intensive Care Units (MICU), Surgical Intensive Care Units (SICU), Pediatric Intensive Care Units (PICU), Burn Units, Trauma Center, Stroke Center among other units.
- Quality and affordable rehabilitation centers and nursing homes for long-term care, recovery and support of our vulnerable population.
- We shall encourage vocation to and provide training for existing Medical and Allied Health Care Professionals: medical doctors, osteopathic physicians, dentists, optometrists, pharmacists, nurses, nurse practitioners, physician assistants, therapists: occupational, speech, physical, chiropractors to bring them in line with the 21st century standards and expectations.
- We shall intensify the implementation of programs to educate the masses on preventive Medicine. We shall promote the regulation of our pharmacies and flow of unauthorized use of prescription drugs and controlled substances and encourage people to see a physician to obtain needed prescriptions and improve follow-up.
- We shall work for the integration of free HIV Clinics and Free Health Clinics and promote the active surveillance and treatment of tuberculosis, typhoid, cholera and emerging diseases, including malaria prevention and treatment and its early detection through sponsored research in our Universities.
- Healthcare workers will be protected and incorporated in community health clinics at the local government level for the more efficient delivery of health care.
- We shall create a Public health advisory council with expertise in different fields of medicine and public health and provide a report and recommendation within six months of our administration to the government on the state of health in Imo State and the way forward.

- A comprehensive state of the art electronic birth and death registry will be established and we shall partner with world class academic institutions to develop and enhance the capacity of our educational sector to provide training to public health and health care professionals.
- The primary health care delivery system will be reactivated and maternal and child care, infectious diseases control, social, mental and environmental health services will be integrated into the system thus enhancing the capacity of community health care centers to deliver a range of preventive and basic curative services to the people of Imo State.
- We shall introduce technological advancements to support data collection and dissemination and develop a public health system that is sensitive to emerging and re-emerging diseases using the revitalized public health network of community health centers.

Show the light and the people will find the way. We will instill accountability in all government endeavors. We shall promote ethics and fiscal responsibility and devise simple ways to promote job creation to improve the economy. **Economic Development** shall be the cornerstone of our policy. **Growing a Sustainable Agro-Economy, Electricity, Water and Basic Necessities** will be promoted while **Energy, Environmental Preservation and Waste Management, Catering to The Vulnerable Population: Seniors and the Disabled** will take the pride of place in our government with **Social Security and Welfare, Women, Children, Youth** and the restoration of **Family Values** at the top of our agenda. **Industrialization, Infrastructural Development, Pension and Wages** will be pursued with vigor. A conscious policy of computerization will be undertaken in all spheres of government endeavor (from land registration, property values and ownership) with a programmed retraining of all government workers and new hires. We intend to place the state at the forefront of **Technology** bolstered with new programs in **Urban Renewal and Housing**

Schemes, with **True Rehabilitation of Roads** you can see and believe in. There will be a vigorous and conscious effort to tackle the problems of **Security and Crime Control** in an effort to redevelop and encourage **Tourism** in Imo State.

We believe that these objectives are achievable within a four year term of office. If we cannot nurture and groom a younger generation to take over from us after four years, then we have failed in our mission. One term is enough. For once let us give men of integrity the opportunity to serve our people and Imo State. Long live Imo State, Long live Nigeria.

CHAPTER 9

INEC AND SUPPLEMENTARY ELECTIONS IN NIGERIA
DR. S. OKECHUKWU MEZU, *pro se* V INEC

IN THE FEDERAL HIGH COURT OF NIGERIA
IN THE OWERRI JUDICIAL DIVISION
HOLDEN AT OWERRI
SUIT NO: FHC/OW/CS/135/11

BETWEEN:
DR. SEBASTIAN OKECHUKWU MEZU
        PLAINTIFF/APPLICANT
AND
INDEPENDENT NATIONAL ELECTORAL COMMISSION (INEC)
        DEFENDANT/RESPONDENT

MOTION ON NOTICE

BROUGHT PURSUANT TO ORDER 26 RULES 1, 2 AND 3 ORDER 56 RULE 8 OF THE FEDERAL HIGH COURT RULES, 2009, AND UNDER THE INHERENT JURISDICCTION OF THIS COURT.

TAKE NOTICE that this honourable court shall be moved on Thursday the 26th day of May 2011 in hour of 9:00 o'clock in the forenoon or so soon thereafter when the applicant or Counsel on his behalf may be heard praying this court for:

1. "an order abridging the time within which the parties in this case may file their papers or processes in this case."

2. "an order that this matter be given accelerated hearing"

And for such further order(s) as the Court may deem fit to make in the circumstances.

Dated this 17th day of May 2011
Dr. S. Okechukwu Mezu
Mezuville, Emekuku,
Owerri North LGA, Imo State

ADDRESS FOR SERVICE

Defendant
Independent National Electoral Commission
INEC State Headquarters
Port-Harcourt Road

IN THE FEDERAL HIGH COURT OF NIGERIA
IN THE OWERRI JUDICIAL DIVISION
HOLDEN AT OWERRI
SUIT NO: FHC/OW/CS/135/11

BETWEEN:
DR. SEBASTIAN OKECHUKWU MEZU
          PLAINTIFF/APPLICANT
AND
INDEPENDENT NATIONAL ELECTORAL COMMISSION (INEC)
          DEFENDANT/RESPONDENT

AFFIDAVIT IN SUPPORT OF THE MOTION AND OF URGENCY

Petitioner herein, Dr. S. Okechukwu Mezu, respectfully seeks this Honourable Court's intervention in equity, and espectfully aver and do hereby make oath and state as follows:

1. That the Petitioner is a resident of Imo State, and a citizen of Nigeria and the Deputy Gubernatorial Candidate, Congress for Progressive Change (CPC) in the Imo State Gubernatorial Elections held on April 26, 2011. The Petitioner is a registered voter in Imo State and voted in the Governorship election of April 26, 2011. The Petitioner is male, adult, a Christian, a Publisher and Businessman and resides at Emekuku, Owerri North LGA, Imo State, Nigeria.

2. That the Respondents are the members of the Independent National Electoral Commission and have offices in Owerri, Imo State, Nigeria.

3. That pursuant to its authority under the Electoral Act of 2006, the Independent National Electoral Commission ("INEC") set the date for the gubernatorial election in Imo

State as April 26, 2011.

4. That pursuant to section 178(2) of the Constitution of Nigeria, elections to the office of Governor of a State, "are to be held on a date not earlier than sixty days and not later than thirty days before the expiration of the term of the office of the last holder of that office."

5. That as the term of the current Governor of Imo State, Ikedi Ohakim, expires at 12 p.m. on May 29, 2011, the INEC was required to set the date of the election as no later than April 29, 2011.

6. That the original election, which took place on April 26, 2011, fulfilled this constitutional mandate.

7. That the election was scheduled to take place on April 26th in all 27 Local Government Areas in Imo State.

8. That however, the INEC has ruled the results of the election "inconclusive" in the four Local Government Areas, those four being Ngor-Okpalla, Mbaitoli, Oguta and Ohaji/Egbema.

9. That the Plaintiff/Applicant has filed originating summons in this case wherein are raised triable issues.

10. That the subject matter of the originating summons is the constitutionality or otherwise of the supple-mentary elections scheduled by INEC on May 6, 2011 within the thirty (30) days to the expiration of the term of the incumbent Governor which period is prohibited by Federal Constitution of Nigeria.

11. That the new Governor of Imo State elected on May 6, 2011 during this prohibited period in a "supplementary election" alien to the Federal Constitution of Nigeria will be sworn in on May 29, 2011.

12. That it is in the public interest and in the interest of jurisprudence and constitutional development of the nation for this matter to be sorted out before the swearing in of the new Governor of Imo State on May 29, 2011.

13. That the circumstances of this case call for the treatment of this case with some urgency

14. That the justice of the case will be best met if time is abridged for the filing of processes and hearing of the case accelerated.

15. That the Defendant will not be prejudiced if this application is granted.

16. That the Plaintiff makes this Oath in good faith believing the contents to be true and correct to the best of his knowledge, information and belief and in accordance to the Oaths Act 2004.

Dr. S. Okechukwu Mezu
Deponent

SWORN TO AT THE FEDERAL HIGH COURT
REGISTRY, OWERRI, IMO STATE, NIGERIA
THIS 17th DAY OF MAY 2011

BEFORE ME
COMMISSIONER FOR OATHS

Chief Registrar Federal High Court Owerri

IN THE FEDERAL HIGH COURT OF NIGERIA
IN THE OWERRI JUDICIAL DIVISION
HOLDEN AT OWERRI
SUIT NO: FHC/OW/CS/135/11

BETWEEN:
DR. SEBASTIAN OKECHUKWU MEZU
          PLAINTIFF/APPLICANT
AND
INDEPENDENT NATIONAL ELECTORAL COMMISSION (INEC)
          DEFENDANT/RESPONDENT

ADDRESS IN SUPPORT OF APPLICATION INTRODUCTION

This address is in support of the application before this honourable court for abridgement of time and for accelerated hearing. Brought pursuant to order 26 Rules 1, 2 and 3, Order 56 Rule 8 of the Federal High Court Rules 2009 and under the inherent jurisdiction of this court, requesting the court's order granting accelerated hearing of this suit and for such further order or other orders as this honourable court may deem fit to make in the circumstances. The application is supported by a sixteen (16) paragraph affidavit and the Plaintiff/Applicant relies on all the paragraphs.

ISSUE FOR DETERMINATION

Whether this court is vested with the powers to grant this application?

LEGAL ARGUMENT

Further to the issue for determination, we contend that this honourable court is vested with the inherent powers to grant this application and the provisions of Order 26 Rules 1, 2, and 3 and Order 56 Rule 8 also permit this court to grant this application.

The Petitioner also contends that this honourable court has ample discretion to grant an application of this nature, vide NEPA v ONYEKANMI (1992) 4 NWLR (237) at page 637 Ratio 3.

CONCLUSION

The Petitioner based on the foregoing respectfully urges the honourable court to grant this application in the interest of justice and the development of jurisprudence.

Dated this 17 day of May 2011

Dr. S. Okechukwu Mezu
Plaintiff/Applicant
Mezuville, Emekuku,
Owerri North LGA, Imo State

ADDRESS FOR SERVICE
Plaintiff:
Dr. S. Okechukwu Mezu
Mezuville, Emekuku,
Owerri North LGA, Imo State

Defendant

Independent National Electoral Commission
INEC State Headquarters
Port-Harcourt Road
Owerri, Imo State

IN THE FEDERAL HIGH COURT OF NIGERIA
IN THE OWERRI JUDICIAL DIVISION
HOLDEN AT OWERRI

SUIT NO:FHC/OW/CS/135/11
BETWEEN:

DR. S. OKECHUKWU MEZU
PLAINTIFF

INDEPENDENT NATIONAL ELECTORAL COMMISSION
DEFENDANT

FURTHER POINTS AND AUTHORITIES IN SUPPORT OF THE PETITION

Rather than count the ballots cast on April 26, 2011, and then certify the winner of the gubernatorial election as the person winning the most such votes, as is its statutory and constitutional duty, INEC has abdicated that duty and chosen instead to declare that duly held election inconclusive. Rather than ensure that election is honored, INEC wants to hold another, untimely and improper partial election. Of course, if INEC can call the first election inconclusive, it can do the same even with the second and third such election, until the results are congenial.

INEC has failed to identify what rendered the proper election inconclusive. The word "inconclusive" means the results are uncertain or unsettled. In an election, though, the results are matter of arithmetic; simply count the votes, and the results are reached. An inconclusive election only arises when all the votes are not counted. INEC has provided no explanation for why votes could not be counted from the April 26, 2011 election. Instead, it has ordered a supplementary election in selected portions of Imo State, without justification and without authority to do so.

I. Any Election on May 6th is Unconstitutional

The timing of gubernatorial elections is specifically controlled by constitutional mandate. The Nigerian Constitution, at Section 178(2), states that,"An election to the office of Governor of a State shall be held on a date not earlier than sixty days and not later than thirty days before the expiration of the term of office of the last holder of that office. " The words "shall be held" contain no room for variance. As the Merriam-Webster dictionary states, the word "shall is used in laws, regulations, or directives to express what is mandatory." In all forms of statutory construction, the word "shall" has always been held to mean mandatory-- the term is not flexible. See, for example, Greenweb Ltd v Wandsworth London Borough Council, [2008] EWCA Civ 910, [2008] All ER (D) 420 (Jul), (Approved judgment)("There was no ambiguity in the word 'shall', or in the phrase 'it shall be assumed that ... '. The assumption was mandatory."); and Fiona Trust & Holding Corporation and others v Privalov and others,[2007] EWCA Civ 20, [2007] 1 All ER (Comm) 891, [2007] 2 Lloyd's Rep 267 ("a stay must be granted, in the light of the mandatory 'shall' in s 9(4). It is this mandatory provision which is the statutory enactment of the relevant article)a stay must be granted, in the light of the mandatory 'shall' in s 9(4). It is this mandatory provision which is the statutory enactment of the relevant article. . . .")(emphasis supplied).

Under the Constitution, then, there is a mandatory 30-day period for gubernatorial elections. The current gubernatorial term expires on May 29, 2011. Thus, the election was required to occur sometime in April. The date INEC originally scheduled, April 26, 2011, the date when the election actually occurred, was near the end of the constitutionally permissible period. The date scheduled for the supplementary election, May 6, is a week beyond the permissible time. Allowing such an election would require that the express language of the Constitution be ignored. In our electoral system, jiust as in, for example, the system in the United Kingdom, the timing of elections is quite significant, and the constitutional scheme must be adhered to closely and rigorously. See, for example, Burke v. Patterson and Another, Queens Bench Division, [1986] NI 1 (" The writ requiring the Chief Electoral Officer to conduct the election "according to law" requires him to conduct proceedings in accordance with the provisions of the legislation. The date upon which he can fix the holding of a poll is prescribed within the narrow limits of rule 1 of the Parliamentary Elections Rules in Schedule 1 to the Representa-tion of the People (Northern Ireland) Regulations 1983. These provisions are mandatory and Parliament intended that they be strictly observed.")

One potential response might be, though, that the Constitution was speaking only of the original election, not the supplementary one. This is quite true, because the Constitution only contemplates one, single, original election. There is to be "an election" scheduled, see Constitution Section 178(1), not multiple elections. The plural is not used in the Constitution because only one election is allowed. The remedy for difficulties counting the votes in that first election is to try harder to do so, not to ignore the first election.

In Tunisia recently for instance, it was observed that three of the most significant problems with their current Constitution and the holding of elections include: timing of the presidential election; presidential versus parliamentary elections; and eligibility criteria for presidential elections. Of interest here is the timing of the Presidential Election. The most obvious problem with their Constitution pertains to the timeframe for holding presidential elections. Under Article 57 of their Constitution, elections must be held within 45 to 60 days from the date of the appointment of an interim President. This corresponds to the length of the mandate of the interim President, Fouad Mebazaa, the Speaker of the Chamber of Deputies, who was sworn in as interim President on 15 January 2011. As stipulated in their Constitution, most legal experts explain that this means that a presidential election ought to be held no later than 15 March 2011 even if it leaves them insufficient time to reform their Electoral Code, which is necessary to increase the likelihood that elections will be genuinely democratic.

II. No Statutory Authority for Supplementary Elections

Elections are not matters to be taken lightly; they are at the core of our nation's political system. They must be free, fair, and governed by statute. Statutory commands must be followed carefully. INEC, in particular, has a special obligation to the Electoral Law of 2006, the statute that regulates and determines INEC's constituency. See Electoral Law of 2006, Part I. Unless the statute allows for a change to election procedures, there must not be such a change. See Burke v. Patterson and Another, Queens Bench Division, [1986] NI 1("[electoral] provisions are mandatory and Parliament intended that they be strictly observed.").

The Electoral Law quite carefully sets out the limited circumstances in which a replacement election may be called, and "inconclusive" results are not among those very limited circumstances. Electoral Law Part IV, Section 54(2) states that

Where the votes cast at an election in any constituency or polling station exceeds the number of registered voters in that constituency or polling station, the election for that constituency or polling station shall be declared null and void by the Commission and another election shall be conducted at a date to be fixed by the Commission.

Similarly, in Part IV, Section 71, the Electoral Law states that

> Where two or more candidates poll equal number of votes being the highest in an election, the Returning Officer shall not return any of the candidates and a fresh election shall be held for the candidates on a date to be appointed by the Commission.

These two provisions are the only two allowing what is in effect a new election, after cancelling out the first one. Their existence shows our nation's legislators contemplated the possibility that elections might need to be nullified after being held in certain very extraordinary situations, but that they carefully selected only those two where such remedy was called for. Those situations are, first, where there truly is a tie after all votes are carefully counted; and second, where there was clear fraud, of the sort often referred to as "stuffing the ballot."

The first situation (a tie) clearly has no application in the current situation in Imo State. As for the second, INEC has not found that in any of the "inconclusive" areas that there was ballot stuffing. There was no announcement that too many votes were cast. There was no decision that the elections there were null and void. Instead, what INEC simply announced the results were inconclusive, with no further attempts to define or explain that term.

"Inconclusive" means just that-- a conclusion was not reached. Yet there is no doubt that voters cast their ballots in those five disputed areas. If the results are "inconclusive," that cannot mean anything but an inability to count the votes that were cast. INEC has not and cannot explain that why those votes cannot be counted. Accordingly, the only remedy available to save the legitimacy of democracy in Imo State and Nigeria as a whole is to declare unconstitutional the announced supplementary election, and if INEC determines that the Imo State Gubernatorial Elections are "inconclusive" the only option is for INEC to cancel the entire gubernatorial election and follow constitutional guidelines in arranging new elections.

III. Allowing Supplementary Elections Will Undermine Our Democratic Institutions

An electoral system relies on the integrity of its voting procedures. More than that, it relies on the public's ability to trust in that integrity. Whatever the motives for INEC declaring the results of a validly held election to be inconclusive, thus rendering the election itself a nullity in significant portions of Imo State, the result of that declaration must be to undermine the public's trust in the integrity of the electoral system. The message to the public is that their votes may be arbitrarily rejected. The message is that rather than count votes, the powers that be may choose to instead reject the results as "inconclusive." The message is that, implicitly, results those powers do not like will be rejected for no stated reason. This is not the way a democratic electoral system must work. A democratic electoral system requires "that the courts should strive to give effect to the will of the electorate and to preserve an election. . . . "Fitch v Stephenson and others; In the matter of the Representation of the People Act 1983, [2008] EWHC 501 (QB), [2008] All ER (D) 13 (Apr), (Approved judgment).

IV. Jurisdiction certainly rests with the Federal High Court

Under section 251. (1) "Notwithstanding anything to the contained in this Constitution and in addition to such other jurisdiction as may be conferred upon it by an Act of the National Assembly, the Federal High Court shall have and exercise jurisdiction to the exclusion of any other court in civil causes and matters - (p) the administration or the management and control of the Federal Government or any of its agencies;"

A Professor of Law, Chidi Odinkalu, like so many others, recently, expressed worries over the scheduled May 6 supplementary gubernatorial election in Imo State, saying it would render section 178(2) of the 1999 Constitution nugatory. According to him, "in ordering supplementary elections to take place on May 6 in four out of 27 local government areas in Imo State, following what it described as "inconclusive elections" for the office of governor in Imo State on April 26, Prof Attahiru Jega's INEC will be manifestly acting contrary to law and without lawful authority or justification.

Vide: "Don faults planned supplementary guber election in Imo (*Vanguard*, May 2, 2011)"

http://www.vanguardngr.com/2011/05/don-faults-planned-supplementary-guber-election-in-imo/

Olisa Agbakoba, SAN, of HURILAWS weighed in also by saying that some Judges would even be minded to issuing an injunction restraining the holding of the "supplementary elections" of May 6, 2011 in Imo State. It is also instructive that All Progressives Grand Alliance (APGA) approached a Federal High Court Judge, Justice Bilikisu Aliyu, on May 5, 2011 in Abuja seeking to stop the supplementary governorship election of May 6, 2011. The Federal Court was unable to sit that day.

The APGA Attorney, Ume, argued that Governor Ohakim, the current governor of Imo State took the oath of allegiance and oath of office on May 29, 2007. Thus, any valid election, declaration of result and return to that office ought to have been concluded on or before April 29, 2011. "It is interesting to note that though Section 178 (3) of the constitution of the Federal Republic of Nigeria, 1999 (as amended) grants the Commission power to extend time for nomination of candidates for election to the office of the governor of a state, same constitution denies the commission the power to hold election and return a candidate to that office on any date not lesser than 30 days to the expiration of the term of office of the last holder of the office."

According to him, "in ordering supplementary elections to take place on May 6 in four out of 27 local government areas in Imo State, following what it described as "inconclusive elections" for the office of governor in Imo State on April 26, Prof Attahiru Jega's INEC will be manifestly acting contrary to law and without lawful authority or justification.' He further inferred that "sadly and patently unfortunately, the Commission arrogated to itself an "extra time" disallowed by the Constitution and the Electoral Act of 2010. "An election to the office of the Governor…", may also infinitely mean "any election," be it "supplementary", "spillover", "residual", "substantive", "re-run", "runoff", "by-election" etc. Besides, the election of April 26, 2011 is inconclusive, meaning that the election had not been completed and no winner emerged. It is also wrong to supplement an inconclusive process. Allowing such a result would have incalculable and irreparably adverse effect on Nigerian democracy. It not only would place the legitimacy of the future governor of Imo State under a cloud, but would make all future elections in Nigeria subject to disrepute and objects of distrust.

Accordingly, the only remedy available to save the legitimacy of democracy in Imo State and Nigeria as a whole is to declare unconstitutional the announced supplementary election, and if INEC determines that the Imo State Gubernatorial Elections are "inconclusive" the only option is for INEC to cancel the entire gubernatorial election and follow constitutional guidelines in arranging new elections.

Respectfully submitted,
Dr. S. Okechukwu Mezu, Plaintiff/Applicant

Dated this 25th day of May 2011

TABLE OF AUTHORITIES

Nigerian Constitution 1999
http://www.nigeria-law.org/ConstitutionOfTheFederalRepublicOfNigeria.htm

The Nigerian Constitution, at Section 178(2)
Electoral Law of 2006, Part I; Part IV, Section 71; Part IV, Section 54(2)

Fitch v Stephenson and others; In the matter of the Representation of the People Act 1983, [2008] EWHC 501 (QB), [2008] All ER (D) 13 (Apr), (Approved judgment).

Burke v. Patterson and Another, Queens Bench Division, [1986] NI 1("[electoral] provisions are mandatory and Parliament intended that they be strictly observed.").

Burke v. Patterson and Another, Queens Bench Division, [1986] NI 1 (" The writ requiring the Chief Electoral Officer to conduct the election "according to law" requires him to conduct proceedings in accordance with the provisions of the legislation. The date upon which he can fix the holding of a poll is prescribed within the narrow limits of rule 1 of the Parliamentary Elections Rules in Schedule 1 to the Representation of the People (Northern Ireland) Regulations 1983. These provisions are mandatory and Parliament intended that they be strictly observed.")

Fiona Trust & Holding Corporation and others v Privalov and others, [2007] EWCA Civ 20, [2007] 1 All ER (Comm) 891, [2007] 2 Lloyd's Rep 267

Greenweb Ltd v Wandsworth London Borough Council, [2008] EWCA Civ 910, [2008] All ER (D) 420 (Jul), (Approved judgment)

"Don faults planned supplementary guber election in Imo (Vanguard, May 2, 2011)"
http://www.vanguardngr.com/2011/05/don-faults-planned-supplementary-guber-election-in-imo/

CHAPTER 10

THE LOUD DRUMS OF CIVIL WAR ARE SOUNDING IN NIGERIA:
No Six Year Term for President and Governors

(Being the text of a press release on July 29, 2011 by Dr. S. Okechukwu Mezu, Congress for Progressive Change (CPC), Deputy Gubernatorial Candidate Imo State 2011 Elections)

The proposed bill from President Goodluck Jonathan for a Six Year term for state Governors and the President (whether motivated by selfish reasons or not) is a totally unnecessary distraction and a disingenuous misplacement of priorities.

A new macabre dance of death has commenced in the Nigerian nation as nationals of one ethnic group rise up against another and sometimes against themselves, as Muslim clerics issue threats of war against Christians and Christian clergy respond that no one has a monopoly of violence. This appears to be a replay of the events that preceded the Nigeria-Biafra War (1967-1970), a war that was long in duration, murderous in intensity, cruel in its execution, disastrous in its consequences and long lasting in its humiliating effects on the Igbos who were vanquished and continue to suffer infrastructural neglect and political relegation nearly fifty years after. No nation survives a civil war two times. The times call for reason and for the leaders and the people to rise above selfishness and bigotry. Yes, the call for a six-year term for the President and the State Governors is an unnecessary distraction in Nigeria where most of those in government came to power through election rigging, multiple thumb-printing of ballots by individuals, killing and maiming of political opponents, mayhem by private armies under the control of political war lords, disenfranchisement of voters through doctored electoral registers, the late arrival of voting materials, multiple copies (sometimes nineteen) of originals of Form EC8A that records the votes cast at the booth, a Form EC8A that never ceases to metamorphose from the voting booth in its journey to various levels of collation centers [Form EC8B, EC8C, etc.] where the votes for parties and individuals change as money changes hand from riggers to Presiding officers, to Electoral Officers and Returning officers, where presiding officers and polling agents sell and buy unused ballot papers, where the number of votes cast exceed the number in the voters' register and armed irate youths surround a polling booth or a collation center until they extract the result they want, where those who kill and maim in the name of politics are freed immediately to walk the streets and continue their mayhem during the next round of elections a week later. Most of those who were elected are intelligent beings and they know how they came to be winners.

There are several cases challenging the results of the various elections [Presidential, Senatorial, House of Representatives, Gubernatorial and State Houses of Assembly] in various Election Tribunals. Very few of them have been adjudicated. What is the urgency to introduce a bill to change the tenure of the President and State Governors from two terms of four years to a single term of six years barely three months after a heavily disputed and seriously flawed election. The Independent National Election Commission should be busy prosecuting those who contravened electoral laws with a view to banning them from future elections if found guilty and should stop talking about preparations for the next election. The President should wait and rather introduce a bill to correct the short-comings in the last elections instead of promoting term elongation. What a misplaced sense of priorities in a nation (one of the richest in the world in human and natural resources) where there are no roads, no electricity, no water to drink, no good hospitals for the sick, no security of life and property, no reliable means of trans-portation – a nation with a decaying educational system, little or no respect for human life, a nation with the highest rate of youth unemployment in the world, where graduates line the streets in their thousands hawking handkerchiefs made in Thailand and impure "pure" water encased in sachets that sicken the thirsty and pollute the environment.

What is the urgency for term elongation for the President and State Governors who find it difficult to pay the poor, lean and hungry looking civil servant a paltry proposed minimum wage of N18,000 (Naira about $120 US Dollars) a month. Some State Governors in addition to their salaries and allowances have a harem of sometimes two hundred Assistants and Special Assistants (of little known specialty) each on salaries of over N500,000 a month plus allowances and fringe benefits. The Governors themselves are entitled to extra budgetal yearly security votes that hover around N5 billion (Naira) for most Governors and as much as N18.9 billion (Naira) for one State Governor. These they use as they please and at their sole discretion. Some utilize these votes rationally for security, while many others use them to buy multi-million dollar mansions in America, Britain and France, Five Star Hotels in Dubai in the Middle East and Durban in South Africa. Members of the National Assembly earn a self-allocated mouth-watering sum of over N100,000,000.00 (Naira) a month and arrogate to themselves the function of the Executive improperly awarding contracts to themselves and executing (when attempted) the projects through their cronies.

Elections will never be free and fair in Nigeria as long as these anomalies subsist as many of the unemployed will do anything – rig elections, kill opponents, maim non-supporters, blackmail other candidates, kidnap their relations - to be able to earn the salary of a local government chairman, a member of the State House of Assembly, or National Assembly (Senate and House of Representatives). The interest of some of these vampires is not good government or governance but the looting of the National Treasury. Part-time or full-time Legislators on a salary of around N500,000.00 to N1 million Naira a month would make the post unattractive to carpetbaggers and opportunists and attractive only to those who really want to serve the state and the nation.

Rather than sending immediately to the National Assembly a bill for term elongation, President Goodluck Jonathan should patiently wait for the Election Tribunals to complete their work, then summon a Sovereign National Conference of the various nationalities, zones and/or ethnic groups in Nigeria with a view to their deliberating on the problems of the nation, the terms of continued union (which is eminently desirable) and proffer solutions, social and constitutional, for submission to the National Assembly as imperfect as it is [since the members do not really represent the wishes of the common people of Nigeria] for promulgation into Law as the Amended Constitution of the Federal Republic of Nigeria. Long Live the Federal Republic of Nigeria! Long Live Black Africa.

CHAPTER 11

A BEFITTING MONUMENT FOR CHUKWUEMEKA ODUMEGWU OJUKWU

"Would Dr. Nnamdi Azikiwe have seceded from Nigeria and declared Biafra's Independence if he were in control of the situation. The answer is definitely NO. Would Dr. Azikiwe have worked out an accommodation under the Aburi Accord that projected a Confederation. The answer is definitely YES. General Ojukwu is General Ojukwu and Zik of Africa is Zik of Africa and never, never the twain shall meet. The above is a veiled and indirect response to the entreaty from John Okiyi viz: "I will write Dr. Mezu to weigh in and give us his honest view [about Dr. Azikiwe and General Ojukwu]. Our elders are still alive and can guide us." There will be time to talk about Ojukwu, the war and Ojukwu's return to Nigeria. I was privileged to hold a private and extended discussion with him after his return from exile. It would be inappropriate to delve into those discussions at this time." quoted from *"Dr. Nnamdi Azikiwe,"* by Dr. S. Okechukwu Mezu, http://eboeville.ning.com/

After writing the above on November 16, 2011, little did I know then that Chukwuemeka Odumegwu Ojukwu, born November 4, 1933 would die ten days later on 26 November 2011.

What would have been the nature and shape of my life, my forty-three years of marriage to my wife, Dr. Rose Ure Mezu, our family, the number of children (ten) we have? What direction would life have taken me, my family, the family of Dr. S. Okechukwu and Dr. Rose Ure Mezu, if, if my life and that of Chukwuemeka Odumegwu Ojukwu had not intersected during the Nigeria-Biafra War?

"Are you married?" asked Ojukwu finally.

"No," replied Dr. S. Okechukwu Mezu. "But I have a fiancée. We were engaged on June 10, 1968."

"You must get married immediately," continued Ojukwu. "I am sending you to Abidjan, Ivory Coast, as Biafra's Ambassador. You are a young man. I want you to travel with your wife. I have not allowed any Biafran diplomat or elder to travel out with their wife during this war - Dr. Nnamdi Azikiwe, Dr. Kenneth Dike, Dr. Michael Okpara, Dr. Pius Okigbo, Dr. Otue, Sir Louis Mbanefo, Chief C. C. Mojekwu, etc. - If they leave Biafra with their wives, I know they will never come back to Biafra. You are different. You were abroad, joined us from there. I can trust you fully. Tomorrow, the Ministry of Foreign Affairs will prepare your passport and that of your wife and the two of you will leave for Abidjan with the next flight out of Uli Airport. They will also prepare the necessary letters of authority."

General Ojukwu did not even ask for my opinion. He seemed not to care whether I was from Owerri or Onitsha or Nnewi, or Calabar. He knew of my work for Biafra in Paris from all his emmissaries, officers and representatives that came there. He probably did see something in me. Our ideas about the war, our fears about its prosecution were identical. We could really communicate without talking. We were alone all night as I briefed him. We talked extensively, about the war, Europe, his emissaries. He was simple, calm and ponderous. He had no illusions about the daunting tasks ahead and the immense suffering of our people. He knew I would accept. I did accept. I was then twenty-seven years old. He was thirty three. He was equal to the task ahead of him.

That conversation took place early in September 1968 at his Umuahia Bunker. I did not really want to leave Biafra again. I wanted to stay home and fight, fight and die if need be with my people. That was my second trip to the war-torn Biafra. I had made an earlier trip into Biafra in June 1968 in one of the night flights carrying arms to Biafra. I had traveled from Paris to Lisbon, Portugal where with the help of Biafra Special Representative, Mr. Ikpa, I joined a Biafra flight carrying arms to Biafra through Sau Tome. I was the Deputy Director of Biafra Historical Research Society, a pseudo-Biafran Embassy set up by Chief Ralph Uwechue and myself in Paris, Chief Uwechue as the Director, myself as the Deputy Director. Ralph Uwechue before then was the Nigerian Chargée d'Affaires at the Nigerian Embassy in Paris who resigned his appointment and joined the Biafra struggle from the beginning and pulled out with him, the French press and all the goodwill Nigeria had in Paris and with the diplomatic community.

The following day, as I went to arrange for the passports a Nigerian fighter jet shrieked across then came back and strafed us - the civilians below with relish and abandon. Lying low in the trench in front of the ministry, I could have picked out the Algerian pilot if I had a shot gun. I believe about seven people died in and around the Biafra Foreign Office Ministry during that raid. Two Nigerian jets came back in the afternoon that day, bombed again the Foreign Ministry and the Ministry of Information with disastrous casualties. My wife and I were quickly married (September 6, 1968) by Rev. Benjamin Dara,

CSSp at St. Patrick's Catholic Church, Umuokrika, Ahiazu, my wife's home parish without a wedding dress and with about ten close members of both families in attendance. As we left the church, two Nigerian jets flew "ceremonially" past the Church. We learned later that a nearby busy market, Afor Oru, was bombed with disastrous consequences.

On September 10, 1968, a few days later, my wife and I left for Libreville, Gabon, from Uli-Ihiala airstrip, code-named "Annabelle" Airport, celebrated in 1970 in my historical novel: *Behind the Rising Sun* (William Heinemann Publishers, London, 1970). We stayed at Hotel Le Gamba and were received by then President Omar Bernard Bongo, another friend of Biafra. President Houphouet Boigny sent his private jet to pick us up from Libreville to Abidjan. We took along a Ghanaian, Mrs Sapara Grant, who was heading back home from Biafra. For a few weeks, Hotel Ivoire, Room 310, would be a new home for my wife and myself. That same week, my wife and I received the first batch of Biafran kwashiokor children as they arrived from Biafra and we flew them to Bouake and made desperate efforts to find them food and comfort. They spent the night in an elementary school open hall.

Who is Chukwuemeka Odumegwu Ojukwu?

Approximately forty three years ago (in 1967), great challenges confronted the Igbos of Nigeria with the *coup d'etat* of January 15, 1966 led by Chukwuma Kaduna Nzeogwu an outstanding progressive, who was buried with full military honors when killed by those he fought against. His *coup d'etat* was triggered by political lawlessness, uncontrolled looting of the treasury in the political arena and uncontrolled looting and lacing in the streets of Western Nigeria. Unfortunately the Sarduana of Sokoto, Sir Ahmadu Bello, the Prime Minister of Nigeria, Sir Tafawa Balewa and the Finance Minister, Chief Festus Okotie Eboh (among others including military officers)

Nigeria Ojukwu Azikiwe Biafra Beyond the Rising Sun [137]

were killed in the process. The pogrom of Igbos followed in Northern Nigeria beginning in July 1966 – atrocities we would rather not recount but should never forget.

I was then completing my Doctoral dissertation at The Johns Hopkins University, in Maryland. As a young man, I led demonstrations in front of the US State Department in Washington D.C. to protest the murder in the Congo of Prime Minister Patrice Lumumba and the Katanga secession. I believed in Pan-African Unity (in fact organized an International Conference on Pan-Africanism as President of the Organization of African and American Students. The proceedings of that conference were edited by me and published in 1965 by Georgetown University Press as *The Philosophy of Pan-Africanism*.) Beyond Pan-African Unity, we believed in a Pan Black world inspired by William DuBois, Marcus Garvey, Booker T. Washington, Kwame Nkrumah, Nnamdi Azikiwe, Julius Nyerere, and those I celebrated in my book *Black Leaders of the Centuries* published in 1970.

The war broke out in 1967. Biafra and the Igbos were attacked and faced liquidation through starvation and blockade from the sea, the air and the land. Many of us were conflicted. Can a committed Pan-Africanist like me really support the secession of Biafra from Nigeria. For me when the choice became clear, it was immediate. I was offered an appointment as a Senior Diplomat by Chief Simeon Adebo, Nigeria's Representative at the United Nations. After a night in his house and as his guest at the Ambassador's Residence in the elegant suburb of New York, my mind was made up. I must fight for the defense of my people.

I postponed the defense of my Doctoral dissertation which I had written in Paris as an exchange student at the *Ecole Pratique des Hautes Etudes*, a joint program of the University of Paris with The Johns Hopkins University. Together with Ambassador Ralph Uwechue, we founded the Biafra Historical

Research Centre in Paris (a pseudonym for the Biafran Embassy in Europe, from where we organized the steady supply of food and medicine through *Caritas Internationalis*, International Red Cross, *Terre des Hommes, Medicins sans Frontier* for the beleaguered citizens of Biafra. I hereby confess that we also sent planes, arms and ammunition through other sources for the defense of Biafra and its citizens and arranged the passage (through Yaounde and Douala) of six young Igbo Nigerian fighter pilots who had just graduated from a training school in Germany. They formed the nucleus of the Biafran Air Force with Chude Sokei then as the Commander.

I was later appointed by General Ojukwu following the recognition of Biafra by Cote d'Ivoire as the Biafran Ambassador to Ivory Coast and President Houphouet-Boigny with concurrent accreditation to Anglophone West Africa and as an envoy to President Leopold Sedar Senghor of Senegal whose works and life (incidentally) was the subject of my Doctoral dissertation. *Leopold Sedar Senghor et la defense et illustration de la civilization noire* (Paris 1968).

Under Ojukwu, I had the honor and privilege of being a member of the Biafran Delegation to Niamey (Niger Republic) Peace Conference under President Hamani Diori (1968) and the OAU sponsored Addis Ababa (Ethiopia) Conference (1968) under the Chairmanship of Emperor Haile Selassie. This was the final effort by General Ojukwu and General Gowon to settle the conflict at the Conference Table. The night before the Conference, I translated into French and had printed General Ojukwu's speech for simultaneous distribution in French and English following its delivery.

The rest is history and even though General Gowon, a good man, promised *"No Victor, No Vanquished,"* the Igbos were not only defeated but were vanquished and treated as such but their heads were unbowed, and remain unbowed.

DID WE LEARN ANY LESSONS FROM THE BIAFRA WAR?

People in government in Nigeria today on the Local Government level, State Government level and Federal level have lost focus. "*Onye anughi oge eliri mmadu, ji esi ukwu na avo ya*" an Igbo saying insists. *When a grave has no marker, anyone not present during the burial is unable to distinguish the location of the head or the feet.* We, in Imo State, for instance, are worse off today (2011) than we were thirty years ago (1981) under the regime of Chief Samuel O. Mbakwe who incidentally fought in the Biafra War. Then there was pipe borne water every where (Owerri, Orlu, Okigwe). We had Amaraku Power generation plant supplying electricity to the state. We had the Aluminum Extrusion plant at Inyishi, Paint Industry in Mbaise, Shoe Industry at Owerri, Clay and Burnt brick industry at Ezinachi, Golden Guinea Breweries, Ceramics Industry, Glass Industry in the then Greater Imo State. Distributors came from as far as Lagos to buy chicken and eggs from Avutu Poultry. We had a functional education system, a functioning Imo State University, a clean urban environment, functioning hospitals, Imo Newspapers Limited. As Chairman of Imo Newspapers Limited, I raised within six months the circulation from 50,000 to 150,000. Today that newspaper is a relic of the past and unseen at newspaper stands and unread by any one.

These strides made thirty years ago are gone replaced by sub-standard mini generating sets, agents of deadly pollution; those strides are replaced by dry water pipes that have not seen water for years; and of course by family untested boreholes in every well-off home. Children of the well-to-do are now sent to expensive private elementary and high schools or abroad for those who can afford it. The brain drain has assumed alarming proportions. Those, in the diaspora, who dare to go back to their states and come home to help (even on Medical Missions) are either kidnapped or unappreciated. Sons overseas are afraid to go home and bury their parents; dutiful daughters uproot their aged mothers and bring them in desperation to America and overseas for basic medical and health needs that could have been taken care of at a General Medical Practitioner's office.

Who will bell the cat? If we, my dying and receding generation, cannot do so, then all hope is lost for the millions of Igbo and Nigerian children, grandchildren and great grandchildren we have at home and abroad. The fate of the parents, siblings and relations they have at home and abroad becomes more problematic. The situation is even then worse for those at home – university graduates from four years ago who have no job, and worse still no hope; those who have jobs and are never paid and when paid, never on time; the pensioners who suffer degradation to collect their monthly allocation years in arrears stretchered on the back of their son or a relation – and some die on the footsteps of the Government Treasury unable to lift their hands to collect their miserly pay for over thirty years of service to the state and the nation. Civil servants tend to forget that the youthful civil servant of today is the maltreated pensioner of tomorrow. Let us make life better for one another and not create hell, in the words of Albert Camus, for one another: *Nous sommes l'enfer les uns pour les autres.*

We cannot for ever live in the Ivory Tower that is America, London, Paris and Abuja and forget the deplorable and miserable conditions of our people at home, the sick, the homeless, the aged – even the forlorn look of desperation of the unemployed able-bodied. We must make the sacrifice to change the situation at home, in Imo State, in Nigeria, in Africa and the black world. No other group of people and no other nation or group of nations can do it for us.

WHO IS TO BLAME

Nigeria Ojukwu Azikiwe Biafra Beyond the Rising Sun

We appear not to have learned any lessons from the Nigerian-Biafra war. If after two, three, four or more years in office as Head of State of the Country Nigeria or Governor of a State in Igbo, Yoruba, Hausa or Ogoni Land and we cannot build a hospital capable of taking care of a sick Odumegwu Ojukwu or a sick Dr. S. Okechukwu Mezu, then we are a dismal failure and a disgrace to the Biafran cause, our people's cause, the Nigerian cause and the global black aspiration. No amount of eulogies, posturing, obfuscation, gallivanting between Lagos and London can mask one's betrayal of the "Biafran" cause and agenda, the Ojukwu cause.

Blockaded by air, land and sea, Ojukwu and Biafra refined enough fuel stored under the canopies of jungle trees in Obohia in Mbaise. These were the products of make-shift Refineries that moved from place to place as the enclave receded. Today the nation spends billions of Naira importing substandard fuel, further adulterated by greed and avarice

Facing deadly air raids from Russian MIG jets piloted by Algerian and Egyptian mercenaries, Ojukwu's Biafra and University scientists created "*Ogbunigwe*," what Americans today would call a weapon of mass destruction. As the drums of war were sounding, Ojukwu's Biafra was planning the establishment of the University of Science and Technology, Port-Harcourt, mark the emphasis - Science and Technology. Dr. Kenneth was to be the Vice Chancellor and I was to head the Department of French and Modern Languages.

Ojukwu's Biafra tried to keep schools open. Doctors labored night and day to save the dying, the wounded, kwashiokor-stricken children. Surgeries were performed sometimes without anesthesia. Young men and women volunteered, joined the defending forces and risked their lives to save their kith and kin. Today young men and a few women are being trained and paid to kidnap and assassinate their kith and kin. Like Dr. Nnamdi Azikiwe, Chukwuemeka Odumegwu Ojukwu set out to be a true Nigerian who could speak Igbo, Hausa, English and Yoruba but history and circumstances beyond Ojukwu's control forced him to become a symbol of Igbo nationalism, a symbol of the literary Okonkwo in Chinua Achebe's *Things Fall Apart*. Exile in Ivory Coast (Côte d'Ivoire) forced on Ojukwu the knowledge of French, the language of his hosts. Ojukwu retreated to Biafra the same way as Dr. Nnamdi Azikiwe, first elected to the Western House of Assembly in Ibadan, was forced to retreat to Enugu in Eastern Nigeria. He who is rejected by others cannot reject himself is a familiar expression in many languages.

A BEFITTING MONUMENT
FOR CHUKWUEMEKA ODUMEGWU OJUKWU

As we all match through deplorable roads, drive through jumpy pot holes and replicas of moon craters we call macadamized thoroughfares; as we fly in planes dripping with water taking off from air terminals reeking with stench from human and industrial effluents, let us remember that honor to Chukwuemeka Ojukwu is not measured in the number of uncomplaining cows we slaughter, the bags of rice we swallow, the basins of kola nuts we eulogize with and masticate, the volume of foreign wines we drink and "*nkwu enu*" we consume; it is not measured by the weight of large denomination mint Naira notes we donate but by our commitment, re-commitment or neo-commitment to the realization of the aspirations of this young man who, thirty three years old had to rein in Biafran military officers some senior to him and more measured, others his juniors and more volatile. He had to get his father's age mates, or near age mates to work with him and for Biafra. Some of these were larger in size than life itself, some were more intelligent, a few were wiser - Nnamdi Azikiwe, Pius Okigbo, Sir Louis Mbanefo, C. C. Mojekwu, Kenneth Dike, Eyo Ita, Jaja Nwachukwu, Dr. K. O. Mbadiwe, Dr. Otue,

Nigeria Ojukwu Azikiwe Biafra Beyond the Rising Sun [143]

Raymond Njoku, Chief Dennis Osadebay, Sir Francis Akanu Ibiam, Inspector Boniface Ihekuna, Inspector General Okeke, Colonel Njoku, Colonel Nwawo, Chukwuma Kaduna Nzeogwu, General Madiebo, General Philip Effiong, Dr. A. A. Nwafor Orizu, M.C. K. Ajuluchukwu, G.C..M Onyiuke, and so many others - diplomats like O. U. Ikpa (Portugal), Godwin Onyegbula (Foreign Ministry), M. T. Mbu (Foreign Affairs), Emeka Anyaoku (Commonwealth Secretary), Ralph Uwechue (Paris), Dr. S. Okechukwu Mezu (Abidjan), Ignatius Kogbara (London), Austin Okwu (Tanzania), Hyacinth Ugwu (Gabon), Dr. Ifegwu Eke (Information), Okoko Ndem (Propaganda), Sylvester Ugoh (Bank of Biafra), N. U. Akpan, Dr. Otue (Canada) Aggrey K. Orji and Dr. Lemeh (New York), Dr. Aaron Ogbonna (West Germany), etc.

Whom do I mention whom do I leave out: Is it Dr. S. E. Cookey, Prof. Eyo Ita, Prof. Eyo Bassey Ndem, Francis Ellah, J. S. Cookey, Emmanuel Aguma; the unsung Academicians of the Biafra Revolution and the scientists of Biafra Research and Production (RAP) - Prof. Eni Njoku, Dr. Okechukwu Ikejiani, Prof. Gordian Ezekwe, Dr. Nwariaku (Petroleum), Professor Augustine Njoku-Obi (Cholera vaccine). Then, there were the Generals, Officers and fighting men of Biafra: General Philip Effiong, Major-General Alex Madiebo, Brigadier Patrick Amadi, Col. Hilary Njoku, Col. Achibong, Col Achuzie, Col. Ben Gbulie, Brigadier Tony Eze, Brigadier Imo, Col Onwuatuegwu, Col. Nwawo, Col David Ogunewe, Commander Chude Sokei, Wing Commander G. I. Ezeilo, Commodore Anuku. If Chief Chukwuemeka Odumegwu Ojukwu was the head of so many "rebels" (a list that is not exclusive), who then are the patriots?

General Ojukwu instead of receiving monthly Nigerian federal allocation of billions of Naira, received daily dislocation of each and every facility in Biafra through bombardment, air raids, artillery fire. Starvation was used as a powerful weapon of war. Undaunted, General Ojukwu and Biafra conceived and produced the *Ogbunigwe*, a cone shaped, sometimes cylindrical cluster bomb that disperses shrapnel with percussion. It was also used as a ground to ground and ground to air projectile and was used with telling and destructive effect. Ojukwu and the Biafra RAP built airports and roads, refined petroleum, chemicals and materials, designed and built light and heavy equipment, researched on chemical and biological weapons, rocketry and guidance systems, invented new forms of explosives, tried new forms of food processing and technology. Biafra home-made armored vehicle the "Red Devil," celebrated also in my book, *Behind The Rising Sun*, was a red terror in the battle field. The Biafra shoreline was lined with home-made shore batteries and remote controlled weapons systems propelling rockets and bombs. There was also the Biafran Organization of Freedom Fighters [BOFF] led by Colonel Aghanya. These were the "so-called" Biafran rebels who in a space of less than three years, blockaded by land, air and sea, nearly pushed black African science and rocketry into the space age. Nigeria and Africa lost a wonderful opportunity.

We should not also forget their wives who did not know if their husbands would come back from work or war, yes the ordinary men and women, professionals, lawyers, doctors, nurses, teachers, farmers. They are many and innumerable. The Heroes of the Biafran War are many and varied in their contributions and their sacrifices. Let us also not forget Ojukwu's companions in life: Njideka, Stella, Victoria and, of course, his surviving widow Bianca née Onoh and their various children. Let us be kinder to them than we were or have been to Flora Azikiwe, Uche Azikiwe, Victoria Aguiyi-Ironsi and Adanma Okpara, Victoria Mbakwe.

Yes a befitting burial will be measured by how we treat the veterans who fought for and against Biafra, how we honor the dead, their widows, their children; how we honor the amputees, the blind, the sick and the challenged in our society. Above all let us not make promises we cannot keep, propose unconsecrated and unfinished monuments that desecrate the dead. Weep not, my country people, and let it not be said that Ojukwu died when the country needed his services most. Let it rather be said that Chukwuemeka Odumegwu Ojukwu lived and served with all his might when the Igbos and Nigerians needed him most. He stood up and fought for what he believed. He stood for justice. He refused to compromise with injustice. He challenged man's inhumanity to man. Born into wealth, he chose to serve his country as an officer in the Nigerian Army when there was nothing to gain. Faced with the pogrom of his kith and kin, he stood his ground and fought until the last plane left Biafra. **To paraphrase Shakespeare, I come not to bury Ojukwu but to make him live. Let his bravery, courage and sacrifices live after him. May whatever perceived mistakes he made, or we think he made, be forever interred with his bones.**

Just as Ojukwu refused to apologize for the Biafra War of Independence even as he lay dying, Obasanjo and his group have refused to forget their role in the Nigerian Civil War and their victory. Just as General Ojukwu died an unrepentant Biafran, General Gowon, General Danjuma and General Obasanjo, when the time comes, will pass on - almost certainly - without apologies to the Igbos. The real Nigerian will only emerge, if ever, when the principal actors in the Biafra-Nigeria cataclysm are no more.

Finally, "*there will be time to talk about Ojukwu, the war and Ojukwu's return to Nigeria. I was privileged to hold a private and extended discussion with him after his return from exile.* (We held further extended discussions in 2003 following the formation of APGA.) *It would be inappropriate to delve into those discussions at this time.*" Let us allow his gentle and courageous soul to rest in peace.

Dr. S. Okechukwu Mezu, December 2, 2011.

CHAPTER 12

SELECT BIBLIOGRAPHY

Achebe, Chinua. *Christmas in Biafra and other poems.* [1st ed.] Garden City, N.Y., Doubleday, 1973.

Achuzia, Joe O. G. *Requiem Biafra* / by Joe O.G. Achuzia. Enugu, Nigeria : Fourth Dimension Publishers, 1986. [Achuzia was one of the more renowned Biafran field commanders]

Ademoyega, Adewale. *Why we struck : the story of the first Nigerian coup.* Ibadan (Nigeria) : Evans, 1981

Affia, George B. *Nigerian crisis, 1966-1970: a preliminary bibliography.* University of Lagos, Yakubu Gowon Library, 1970.

Aguolu, Christian Chukwunedu. *Nigerian Civil War, 1967-1970; an annotated bibliography.* Boston, G. K. Hall, *1973.*

Akinyemi, A. B. *The British press and the Nigerian civil war : the godfather complex (NIIA monograph series. no. 2).* Oxford University Press, 1979.

Akpan, Ntieyong Udo. *The struggle for secession, 1966-1970; a personal account of the Nigerian Civil War.* London, F. Cass, 1972, c1971

Amadi, Elechi, 1934- . *Sunset in Biafra: a civil war diary.* London, Heinemann Educational, 1973.

Asika, Ukpabi. *No victors, no vanquished.* (Enugu) East-Central State Information Service 1968.

Awolowo, Obafemi. Awo on the Nigerian Civil War. Ikeja, Nigeria : J. West Publications, 1982

Azikiwe, Nnamdi. *Origins of the Nigerian Civil War.* Apapa : Nigerian National Press, 1969

_____. Peace proposals for ending the Nigerian civil war. London : Colusco, 1969.

Cervenka, Zdenek. *The Nigerian war, 1967-1970. History of the war; selected bibliography and documents.* Frankfurt am Main, Bernard & Graefe, 1971.

Chima, Alex. *Future lies in a progressive Biafra: a socio-economic history of the republic of Biafra.* London, Alex Chima, 1968.

Chuku, Gloria. "Igbo Women and Political Participation in Nigeria, 1800s-2005," in *The International Journal of African Historical Studies*, Vol. 42, 2009

Cohen, Robin. *"A greater south": or what might have happened in the Nigerian Civil War.* University of Birmingham, Faculty of Commerce and Social Science, Series C, no. 22. 1971

Collis, William Robert Fitz-Gerald. *Nigeria in conflict.* London, Secker & Warburg, 1970.

Cronje, Suzanne. *The world and Nigeria: the diplomatic history of the Biafran War, 1967-1970.* Sidgwick and Jackson, 22p.

De St. Jorre, John. *The brothers' war; Biafra and Nigeria.* Boston, Houghton Mifflin, 1972.

East-Central State (Nigeria). Ministry of Works, Housing, and Transport. *Report on war damages to roads, bridges, waterworks and equipment in the East Central State of Nigeria.* Enugu, Printed by the Govt. Printer 1970

Eastern Nigeria. Ministry of Information. *Nigerian crisis 1966: (Eastern Nigeria viewpoint).* Enugu, Eastern Nigeria. Ministry of Information. 1966.

Ekwe-Ekwe, Herbert. *The Biafra war : Nigeria and the aftermath.* Lewiston, N.Y., USA : E. Mellen Press, c1990.

Ekwensi, Cyprian. *Divided we stand : a novel of the Nigerian Civil War.* Enugu, Nigeria : Fourth Dimension, 1980.

Emecheta, Buchi. *Destination Biafra : a novel.* London ; New York : Allison & Busby ; New York, N.Y. : Distributed by Schocken Books, 1982

Enonchong, Charles. *I know who killed Major Nzeogwu! : an investigation into the most secret cover-up of the Nigerian Civil War.* Lagos : Century, 1991.

Forsyth, Frederick. *The Making of a Nation: The Biafran story.* Baltimore, Penguin Books [1969]

Forsyth, Frederick. *Emeka.* Edition: Reprinted with corrections 1992. Ibadan, Nigeria : Spectrum Books ; Jersey, Channel Islands, UK : Safari Books (Export), 1992.

Gbulie, Ben. *Nigeria's five majors : coup d'etat of 15th January 1966, first inside account.* Onitsha, Nigeria : Africana Educational Publishers (Nig), c1981

_____. *The fall of Biafra.* Enugu, Anambra State, Nigeria : Benlie, 1989

Graham-Douglas, Nabo B. *Ojukwu's rebellion and world opinion.* London : Galitzine, Chant, Russell and Partners, 1968.

http://www.kwenu.com/igbo/igbowebpages/Igbo.dir/Biafra/books_on_biafra.htm

Idahosa, Patrick E. *Truth and tragedy : (a fighting man's memoir of the Nigerian Civil War)*
Ibadan : Heinemann Educational Books, 1989.

Ike, Vincent Chukwuemeka, 1931- . *Sunset at dawn : a novel about Biafra.* London : Collins and Harvill Press, 1976.

Iroh, Eddie. *The siren in the night.* London : Heinemann, 1982.

_____. *Toads of war.* London : Heinemann, 1979.

Kirk-Greene, A. H. M. (Anthony Hamilton Millard). *Crisis and conflict in Nigeria: a documentary sourcebook.* London, Oxford University Press, 1971.

Lloyd, Hugh G. et al. *The Nordchurchaid airlift to Biafra, 1968-1970. An operations Report.* Copenhagen, 1150 Kobenhavn K., Folkekirkens Nodhjalp, Eksp.: Kobmagergade 26, 1972.

Madiebo, Alexander A. *The Nigerian revolution and the Biafran war.* Enugu, Nigeria : Fourth Dimension Publishers,

1980. [Madiebo was the general officer commanding the Biafran army]

Mezu, Sebastian Okechukwu. *Behind the Rising Sun*. [a historical nove about the Biafran war] London, Heinemann, 1971.

_____ *Nigerian Elections 2007: Chronicle of Shame and Deceit.* Baltimore: Black Acacdemy Press, Inc. 2007.

_____ Tropical Dawn, poems. Buffalo: Black Academy Press, Inc., 1970.

_____. *Leopold Sédar Senghor et la défense et illustration de la civilisation noire.* Paris, Marcel Didier, 1968, 232p

Some Reviews of *Behind the Rising Sun*

_____ "Biafra" Two Radio Talks on the problems of reconciliation and reconstruction on WGR Radio, January, 1970.

_____ "Biafran Prof Talks of War", by Deborah Williams, Buffalo *Courier-Express,* Sunday, August 3, 1969, P. 38.

_____ "Struggle to Survive" review of novel *Behind the Rising Sun,* (BRS) by Norma Reed, *The Cape Times,* (South Africa), April 8, 1971.

_____ "Other New Novels," (BRS) by Tamara Salaman, *The Observer* (London), April 18, 1971.

_____ "An African Looks at War in Biafra" (BRS) by D.A.H., *The Natal* Mercury, June 10, 1971.

_____ "Biafra Novel" (BRS) by David Thomas, *The Star* (Johannesburg) June 26, 1971.

_____ "Novel about Biafra" (BRS) Ross N. Dale, *Baptist Times* London, June 10, 1971.

_____ "The Nice and the Nasty" (BRS) by Phyllis Bentley, *The Yorkshire Post* April 8, 1971.

_____ "New Novels" (BRS), by W. J. Nesbitt, *The Northern Echo* (Durham) April 8, 19 7 1.

_____ "Too Much Like a Boy's Tale of Adventure" (BRS) by D. D. *The Pretoria News* July 7, 1971.

_____ "Behind the Rising Sun" in *Sun* (Melbourne), June 5,

Nigeria Ojukwu Azikiwe Biafra Beyond the Rising Sun [151]

1971.

_____ "The Price of Creation" (BRS) by Derek Stanford, *The Scotsman* (Edinburgh) April 17,1971.

_____ "Behind the Rising Sun", *The Journal,* (Newcastle-upon-Tyne), Apr 17, 1971.

_____ "Summer Season Fiction : Four novels with breath of Life" (BRS) by Leslie Farmer, *Methodist Recorder* (London) August 19, 1971, p. 13.

_____ "Patriots and Profits" (BRS) by Keith Carter, *The Times Educational Supplement* (London) September 24,1971.

_____ "Behind the Rising Sun: Truth is Stranger than Fiction" by David Jowitt, *West Africa* (London) November 5, 1971.

_____ "The Literature of Civil War" (BRS), *The Times Literary Supplement* March 3, 1972, pp. 247-248.

Mezu, S. Okechukwu. "Du Nigeria Oriental à la Republique du Biafra," *Esprit* (Paris) no. 12, December 1969, pp. 787-806

_____ "Towards A Progressive Pan-Africana Studies & Research Program," *Black Academy Review* Vol. 1, No. 2, 1970, pp.74-80

_____ "The Cradles of Modern African Literature," *The Conch"* Vol. 2, No. 1, 1970, pp. 3 - II.

_____ "The Seventies: The Age of Realism for Africa," *The African Scholar,* Vol. 3, No. 1, 1970.

_____ "Economic Stalactites and Stalagmites," *Commissioning of Emekuku Community Bank Nigeria Limited*, June 7, 1991.

_____ "The Life and Times of Ken Saro-Wiwa," *Black Academy Review*, Vol. 7, Nos 1-2, 1996.

_____ "Africa in turmoil: From Political Independence to Economic Slavery," *Black Academy Review*, Vol. 6, Nos 1, Spring, 1995

_____ "Heroes and Villains of the Pan-African Movement," *Black Nationalists: Reconsidering Du bois, Garvey, Booker T & Nkrumah.* S. Okechukwu Mezu & Rose Mezu.

Eds. Baltimore, Black Academy Press, 1999, pp. 109-135.

_____ "Pan-Africanism, Trans-Africa and Beyond," In *Africa and The Diaspora*. Rose Mezu, Ed. Baltimore, Black Academy Press, Inc., 1999, pp. 115-140.

_____ "Le Biafra et la conscience mondiale", Cercle Culturel International de Langue Francaise, Canisius College, Buffalo, New York October 28, 1969.

_____ "Biafra: What Next", Television (One half-hour) program on WBEN-Buffalo, Buffalo Round Table with Dr. Fred Burke, -Dr. Ram Desai & Moderator, January 25, 1970.

Mainasara, A. M. *The five majors : why they struck*. Zaria [Nigeria] : Hudahuda Publishing Co., 1982.

McLuckie, Craig W. *Nigerian Civil War literature : seeking an "imagined community"* Lewiston, NY : E. Mellen Press, c1990.

Mok, Michael. *Biafra journal*. New York, Time-Life Books [1969]

Nafziger, E. Wayne. *The economics of political instability : the Nigerian-Biafran war*
Boulder, Colo. : Westview Press, 1983.

Ngoh, Victor Julius. *The United States and the Nigerian Civil War, 1967-1970 : an analysis of the American policy toward the war*. Ph.D. Thesis, University of Washington, 1982.

Niven, Rex, Sir. The war of Nigerian unity, 1967-1970. Totowa, N.J., Rowman and Littlefield <1971, c1970>.

Nwankwo, Arthur Agwuncha and S. Udochukwu Ifejika. *The making of a nation: Biafra*. London, C. Hurst, 1969.

_____. *Nigeria: the challenge of Biafra*. London, R. Collings, 1972.

Nwapa, Flora. Never again. Trenton, N.J. : Africa World Press, 1992.

Nwankwo, Arthur Agwuncha. *Nigeria: the challenge of Biafra*. London, R. Collings, 1972.

Nweke, G. Aforka. *External intervention in African conflicts : French-speaking West Africa in the Nigerian Civil War, 1967-70.* African Studies Center, Boston University, 1976.

Nwigwe, Henry Emezuem. *Nigeria - The Fall of the First Republic.* London, Motorchild Press, [1972]

Nwoye, S. C. & Ikegbune, E. *Biafrana at Nsukka : a list of materials on the Nigerian Civil War available at the Nnamdi Azikiwe Library* (University of Nigeria, Nsukka).
Nsukka : University of Nigeria Library,1983

Obasanjo, Olusegun. *Not my will.* Ibadan : University Press Ltd., 1990.

_____. *Nzeogwu : an intimate portrait of Major Chukwuma Kaduna Nzeogwu*
PUBLISHER Ibadan : Spectrum Books, 1987.

_____. *My command : an account of the Nigerian Civil War, 1967-1970.* Ibadan, : Heinemann, 1980.

Obikeze, Dan S. and Ada A. Mere. Children and the Nigerian Civil War : a study of the rehabilitation programme for war-displaced children. Nsukka : University of Nigeria Press, 1985.

Odogwu, Bernard, 1936- *No place to hide : crises and conflicts inside Biafra.* Enugu, Nigeria : Fourth Dimension, 1985. [Odogwu was head of Biafra's secret service unit]

Ojukwu, Chukwuemeka Odumegwu, *Because I am involved.* Ibadan : Spectrum Books Ltd., 1989

_____. *Principles of the Biafran revolution : as enunciated by General C. Odumegwu Ojukwu.* Cambridge, Mass. : Biafra Review, 1969

_____. *Biafra; selected speeches and random thoughts of C. Odumegwu Ojukwu, with diaries of events.* New York, Harper & Row, 1969.

Ogbudinkpa, Nwabeze Reuben. *The economics of the Nigerian Civil War and its prospects for national developmment.* Enugu, Nigeria : Fourth Dimension Publishers, 1985.

Ogbemudia, S. O. *Years of challenge*. Ibadan : Heinemann Educational Books, 1991.

Oguntoyinbo, Lekan. "A Passion for Africa," *Diverse Issues in Higher Education*, Vol. 28, May 26, 2011.

Okpaku, Joseph . Ed. Nigeria: dilemma of nationhood - an African analysis of the Biafran conflict. New York, Third Press, 1972.

Oluleye, James J. *Military leadership in Nigeria, 1966-1979*. Ibadan : University Press Ltd., 1985.

O'Malley, Patrick. *"No such country" : footnotes on the Nigerian civil war*. (Zomba) : University of Malawi, History Dept.,1984.

Opia, Eric Agume. *Why Biafra? : Aburi, prelude to Biafran tragedy*. San Rafael, Calif. : Leswing Press, c1972.

Owen, Olly. "Biafran Pound Notes," *Africa*. Vol. 79, 2009.

Ozalla, M. Odogwu. *Ojukwu's new type democracy*. Lagos (Committee of Ibo Intellectuals) 1969

_____. *Ojukwu's "self-determination"; a reappraisal in the light of international politics*. (Apapa, Printed by the Nigerian National Press 1969.

Panter-Brick, S. K. ed. *Nigerian politics and military rule: prelude to the Civil War*.
Lond: University of London; 1970

Parise, Goffredo. *Biafra*. Milano, Libreria Feltrinelli, 1968.

Saro-Wiwa, Ken. *On a darkling plain : an account of the Nigerian civil war*. London : Saros, 1989.

Schabowska, Henryka. *Africa reports on the Nigerian Crisis : news, attitudes and background information : a study of press performance, government attitude to Biafra and ethno-political integration*. Uppsala : Scandinavian Institute of African Studies, 1978.

Shiels, Frederick L. Ed. *Ethnic separatism and world politics*. Lanham, MD : University Press of America, c1984.

Soyinka, Wole. *The Man Died.* 1973.

Stremlau, John J. *The international politics of the Nigerian civil war, 1967-70.* Princeton University Press, c1977.

Sullivan, John R. *Breadless Biafra.* Dayton, Ohio, Pflaum Press, 1969.

Thompson, Joseph E. *American policy and African famine : the Nigeria-Biafra War, 1966-1970* New York : Greenwood Press, 1990.

Uchendu, Egodi. "Recollections of Childhood Experiences during the Nigerian Civil War." *Africa,* Vol. 77, 2007.

Ugobelu, Egbebelu. *Biafra war revisited : a concise account of events that led to the Nigerian civil war.* Atlanta, GA : ProPrints of Atlanta, 1992.

Uku, Skyne R. *The Pan-African movement and the Nigerian civil war.* New York : Vantage, 1978.

United States Congress. House Committee on Foreign Affairs. Subcommittee on Africa.
Report of the Special Coordinator for Nigerian Relief. Hearing, Ninety-first Congress, first session. April 24, 1969. Washington, U.S. Govt. Print. Off., 1969

Urhobo, Emmanuel. *Relief operations in the Nigerian civil war.* Ibadan, Nigeria : Daystar Press, 1978.

Uwanaka, Charles U. *Nigerian civil war : causes, events (1956-1967).* Ebute-Metta : De Mediator Press, 1981.

Uwazurike, Ralph. "Interview with Ralph Uwazurike," by Chinedu Opara. February 3, 2012 http://chukseoluigbo.blogspot.com/2012/02/ralph-uwazuruike-south-east-governors.html

Uwechue, Raph. *Reflections on the Nigerian civil war; facing the future.* With forewords by Nnamdi Azikiwe & Leopold Sedar Senghor. New York, Africana Pub. Corp. 1971.

Waugh, Auberon. *Biafra: Britain's shame.* London, Joseph, 1969.

Wiseberg, Laurie Sheila. *The international politics of relief : a case study of the relief operations mounted during the Nigerian civil war (1967-1970)*. Thesis - University of California, Los Angeles, 1973.

Wiseberg, Laurie S. *The Nigerian civil war, 1967-1970; a case study in the efficacy of international law as a regulator of intrastate violence*. Southern California Arms Control and Foreign Policy Seminar, 1972.

CHAPTER 13

ABOUT THE AUTHOR

Dr. S. Okechukwu Mezu

Background

Dr. S. Okechukwu Mezu was born on April 30, 1941 in Ezeogba, Emekuku, Owerri Imo State. He attended Holy Ghost Juniorate, Ihiala (1954-1956), Holy Ghost College, Owerri (1957-1958) and Holy Family Higher School, Abak (1959-1960). He received an ASPAU Scholarship (African Scholarship Program of American Universities) to Georgetown University, Washington D. C. from where he received a B.A. in French (1964) with minors in German and Philosophy. He obtained an LL.B. with distinction in 1966 from La Salle Extension University, Chicago, Illinois and an M.A. (1966) from the Johns Hopkins University. He obtained a *Diplome d'Etudes* from the University of Paris, *Ecole Pratique des Hautes Etudes,* Sorbonne, France and a Ph.D (1967) in Romance Languages with Distinction in Oral Boards (French and Spanish) from The Johns Hopkins University, Baltimore Maryland. He was Professor of French and Founder and Director African Studies Program at the State University of New York at Buffalo (1969-1973) and visiting Professor at several Universities, SUNY at Albany, SUNY at Old Westbury, Howard University, University of Pittsburgh, The Pennsylvania State University, University Park, etc. He came back to Nigeria on January 15, 1973, was appointed Professor and Chairperson, Department of Modern Languages and Member of the Senate of University of Nigeria (Nsukka) by Professor Kodilinye. He declined the appointment and went to his village, Ezeogba Emekuku, Owerri and established Mezu International Limited in 1973 to help create employment for the people.

In the 1979, he helped found the Imo State branch of the Nigerian Peoples Party (NPP) and as Secretary of the Nigerian Peoples Party (NPP) he helped to elect and install the greatest Governor Imo State has ever had, Governor Samuel Onunaka Mbakwe and other notable names to office. Following the success of the NPP at the polls, he became the Chairman of the Golden Breweries Limited (1979 – 1980) and rehabilitated and revitalized the brewery during their $50 million expansion of the premier brewery in Nigeria and later as chairman of The Imo State Newspapers Ltd, he raised the daily circulation of the *Nigerian Statesman* from 50,000 to 150,000.

He is also a renowned writer, scholar, philanthropist (established Mezu International Scholarship Award for best students in several Secondary Schools). As a publisher, he established Black Academy Press, Inc, (1969) one of the very first black owned academic publishing Companies that set the tone for Africana studies in the Sixties in America. It remains one of the longest standing historic black publishing companies today.

Early political career

He was the Campaign Director, Party Secretary and principal architect of Nigerian Peoples Party (NPP), that won a landslide victory (over 80%) in the Imo State Legislative, Gubernatorial and Presidential Elections in Nigeria in 1979.

Diplomatic Service

When the Biafran war broke out in 1967, due to the recognition of his valuable contributions and genuine patriotism and vibrant activism as a young scholar in the United States and France where he had voluntarily translated volumes of documents for his country into French and other languages. Dr. S. O Mezu was appointed Biafran/Government Special Representative and Ambassador to Abidjan, Ivory Coast (Cote d'Ivoire) at the age of 27 by Colonel Odumegwu Ojukwu and was charged with affairs in Francophone and Anglophone West Africa.

He was co-founder with Ambassador Ralph Uwechue and Deputy Director, Biafra Historical Research Center, Paris, July 1967 – July 1968 then Biafra's semi-official diplomatic mission to France and Europe. He was also Biafran delegate and French expert to various peace delegations to Ivory Coast (President Felix Houphouet-Boigny), Senegal, (President Leopold Sedar Senghor), Gabon (President Albert Bernard Bongo), etc. He was also a Biafran delegate and French expert to various peace Conferences in Niamey, Niger Republic (President Hamani Diori, 1968) and in Addis-Ababa, Ethiopia (Emperor Haile Selassie, 1968).

DR. S. OKECHUKWU MEZU & DR. ROSE URE MEZU

Dr. S. Okechukwu Mezu has been married to Dr. Rose Ure Mezu for forty-three years and they have ten children (eight of them have their Doctorates (some with double doctorates) in Medicine [Cardiology/ Electrophysiology, Pediatrics and Neo-Natology, Internal Medicne and Infectious Diseases, Public Health, Pharmacy and Optometry], in Law and Accountancy, in Electrical and Computer Engineering, Information Sciences; one is finishing his Ph.D in Information Sciences, while the youngest is working towards a Masters in Information Science). The Mezus have also thirteen grand-children. Dr. Rose Ure Mezu, a Professor in the United States, is also a widely published author of numerous literary works about feminism, religion, authentic femininity, ethnic pride. She is a Professor of English and Comparative Literature of international repute deeply respected by her peers and greatly valued by her students, the young minds she shapes in preparation for their roles as future leaders of the African diaspora and the world at large. She has also very active speaking engagements.

Dr. Rose Ure Mezu was the First Lady Commissioner for Social Welfare under the Government of Samuel Onunaka Mbakwe of the Greater Imo State 1979-1983 and the **only** political appointee in the Federation of Nigeria that was never arrested or imprisoned when General Buhari and General Tunde Idiagbon took over the government in 1983. When Dr. Rose Ure Mezu faced the Tribunal headed by General Abdulkarim Adisa (then a Colonel), General Adisa had this to say: *"Please don't come here again. Go home. Abi you no sabi chop or you no wan chop!"* This attests to her honesty, integrity, selfless, wholehearted service and incorruptible nature during her four year tenure as the First Female Commissioner for Social Welfare. She was the only Commissioner in the entire Nigerian Federation who was not sent to jail during the Buhari/Idiagbon regime. She is also the founder of Our Lady's Food Kitchen that feeds the poor, the old and the undeserved. Her published works include among others: *Women in Chains: Abandonment in Love Relationships; Chinua Achebe:The Man and his Works; Hommage to My People* (poems); *History of Africana Women's Literature; Songs of the Hearth*, poems; *Religion and Society; Africa and the Diaspora; Leadership, Culture and Racism*, co-edited with Dr. Burney Hollis and *Black Nationalists: Reconsidering Du Bois, Garvey, Booker T. & Nkrumah* co-edited with Dr. S. Okechukwu Mezu.

Some of the works of Dr. S. Okechukwu Mezu include *The Philosophy of Pan-Africanism*, S. Okechukwu Mezu. ed., Washington, D.C., Georgetown University Press, 1965, 142p; *The Tropical Dawn, poems*, Baltimore, Maryland, 1966; Buffalo, Black Academy Press, Inc., 1970, 60 p.; *Leopold Sédar Senghor et la défense et illustration de la civilisation noire*, S. Okechukwu Mezu. Paris, Marcel Didier, 1968, 232 p.; *Black Leaders of the Centuries*, S. Okechukwu Mezu, & Ram Desai, eds. Buffalo, Black Academy Press, Inc., 1970, 302 p.; *Behind the Rising Sun*, a novel about the Biafran war. S. Okechukwu Mezu. London, William Heinemann, Ltd., 1971, 242p; paper edition (African

Writers Series, No. 113) London, Heinemann Educational Books, Ltd., 1972; *Modern Black Literature*, S. Okechukwu Mezu. ed. Buffalo, Black Academy Press, Inc., 1971; *The Literary Works of Senghor*, S. Okechukwu Mezu. London Heinemann Educational Books, Ltd.,- 1972, 121 p.; *Igbo Market Literature*, S. Okechukwu Mezu. compiler. 5 vols., Buffalo, Black Academy Press, Inc., 1972, 4000 p.; *The Meaning of Africa to Afro-Americans: A Comparative Study Of Race & Racism*, S. Okechukwu Mezu. ed. Buffalo, Black Academy Press, Inc., 1972, 175 p.; *Umu Ejima* (The Twins), S. Okechukwu Mezu. An Igbo adaptation of the Latin play, Menaechmi by Plautus. Owerri, Black Academy Press, 1975, 60p.; *Leopold Sedar Senghor*, by S. Okechukwu Mezu. London: Heinemann, 1973; *Ken Saro-Wiwa: the life and times*, and so many other works.

Cover photo shows General Odumegwu Ojukwu & Dr. S. Okechukwu Mezu in an intimate conversation at Ojukwu's Family House, Enugu, Nigeria, January 23, 2003

www.ingramcontent.com/pod-product-compliance
Lightning Source LLC
Chambersburg PA
CBHW050640160426
43194CB00010B/1748